Volume 37 Number 2 2004

Discourse Processes

A MULTIDISCIPLINARY JOURNAL

Special Issue: Accessibility in Text and Discourse Processing

Guest Editors: Ted J.M. Sanders and Morton Ann Gernsbacher

Contents

First Published by

Lawrence Erlbaum Associates, Inc., Publishers
10 Industrial Avenue
Mahwah, New Jersey 07430

Transferred to Digital Printing 2010 by Routledge
270 Madison Ave, New York NY 10016
2 Park Square, Milton Park, Abingdon, Oxon, OX14 4RN

ISBN 0-8058-9556-6 (pbk)

Publisher's Note
The publisher has gone to great lengths to ensure the quality of this reprint but points out that some imperfections in the original may be apparent.

DISCOURSE PROCESSES, *37*(2), 79–89

Accessibility in Text and Discourse Processing

Ted J.M. Sanders
Utrecht institute of Linguistics UiL OTS
Utrecht University

Morton Ann Gernsbacher
Department of Psychology
University of Wisconsin–Madison

Accessibility is one of the most important challenges at the intersection of linguistic and psycholinguistic studies of text and discourse processing. Linguists have shown how linguistic indicators of referential coherence show a systematic pattern: Longer linguistic forms (like full lexical NPs) tend to be used when referents are relatively low accessible, shorter forms (pronouns and zero anaphora) are used when referents are highly accessible. This linguistic theory fits in nicely with a dynamic view of text and discourse processing: When a reader proceeds through a text, the activation of concepts as part of the reader's representation fluctuates constantly. Hypotheses considering activation patterns can be tested with on-line research methods like reading time or eye-movement recording. The articles in this special issue show how accessibility phenomena need to be studied from a linguistic and a psycholinguistic angle, and in the latter case from interpretation as well as production.

What happens when people read a text or participate in a discourse? Text and discourse processing are dynamic processes during which the reader or listener constructs a cognitive representation of the information in the text or discourse. Even though readers' and listeners' representations are not identical to the information they read and hear, texts and discourses contain many linguistic signals that guide comprehension. These assertions are among the most important results of research on text and discourse processing during the last decades (see, among others,

Correspondence and requests for reprints should be sent to Ted Sanders, Utrecht institute of Linguistics UiL OTS, Utrecht University, Trans 10, NL-3512 JK Utrecht, The Netherlands. E-mail: Ted.Sanders@let.uu.nl

Gernsbacher & Givón, 1995; Graesser, Millis, & Zwaan, 1997; Sanders & Spooren, 2001). The main findings can be summarized as follows:

- Text and discourse processing results in a cognitive representation of the information. The crucial characteristic of this representation is that it shows connectedness. This connectedness can be best characterized as *coherence.*
- The cognitive processes of text and discourse production and interpretation can be modeled as dynamic processes in which activation fluctuates. These process are influenced, or even to a large extent determined, by the linguistic characteristics of the text or discourse.

Before going into more detail on these two findings, we shall first illustrate them with a concrete example (Sanders & Spooren, 2002): that of referential coherence. Referential coherence results from the fact that reference to individuals creates continuity and hence coherence in the text or discourse. The relevant linguistic signals are the references to objects and concepts, and more specifically, the ways in which the reference is realized—through full Noun phrases, pronouns, zero anaphora, and so on.

The following text from Matthews (1994) illustrates how referential coherence structures discourse:

(1) The heaviest human in medical history was Jon Brower Minnoch (b. 29 Sep 1941) of Bainbridge Island, WA, who had suffered from obesity since childhood. The 6-ft-1-in-tall former taxi driver was 392 lb in 1963, 700 lb in 1966, and 975 lb in September 1976. In March 1978, Minnoch was rushed to University Hospital, Seattle, saturated with fluid and suffering from heart and respiratory failure. It took a dozen firemen and an improvised stretcher to move him from his home to a ferryboat. When he arrived at the hospital he was put in two beds lashed together. It took 13 people just to roll him over. (p. 151)

The text's topic, Jon Brower Minnoch, is identified in the first sentence and is referred to in each sentence throughout this segment of text. Here are the referential forms, with ∅ standing for zero-anaphor:

Jon Brower Minnoch (b. 29 Sep 1941) of Bainbridge Island, WA
The 6-ft-1-in-tall former taxi driver
Minnoch
∅
∅
him
he
he
him.

First of all, this list shows that the linguistic indicators for referential coherence are lexical NPs, pronouns, and other devices for anaphoric reference. Second, it appears that the longest referential forms are used in the beginning of the fragment; once the referent has been identified, the pronominal and zero forms suffice. This is not a coincidence. Many linguists have noted this regularity and related it to the cognitive status of the referents. Ariel (1990, 2001), for instance, has argued that this type of pattern in grammatical coding should be understood to guide processing. She has developed an *accessibility theory* in which high accessibility markers consist of less linguistic material and signal the default choice of continued activation. By contrast, low accessibility markers consist of more linguistic material and signal the terminated activation of the current (topical) referent.

It is not hard to see how a linguistic theory like this fits in with a dynamic view of text and discourse processing. For instance, such a dynamic view leads to the expectation that when a reader proceeds through a text, the activation of concepts, facts, and events as parts of the reader's representation fluctuates constantly. So, hypotheses considering activation patterns can be tested with online research methods like reading time, naming, speeded recognition, or eye-movement recording. Eventually, the fluctuating activation patterns settle into a relatively stable memory representation.

Several discourse comprehension models are based on these insights and empirical findings, such as the Structure Building Framework (Gernsbacher, 1990), the Landscape Model of Reading (Gaddy, van den Broek, & Sung, 2001; van den Broek, Young, Tzeng, & Linderholm, 1998), and the Construction–Integration model (Kintsch, 1998). Questions of how exactly this activation fluctuates and how the activation is influenced by the linguistic characteristics of the text or discourse are currently major research questions, which are partly addressed in contributions to this issue.

Now that we have illustrated the principles of referential coherence and accessibility in text linguistics and discourse processing, we can move on by specifying some major ideas of accessibility.

LINGUISTICS: THE SYSTEM AND USE OF REFERENTIAL SIGNALS

As explained earlier, Mira Ariel has developed an Accessibility marking scale (Ariel, 1990), from low to high accessibility markers:

(2) Full name > long definite description > short definite description > last name > first name > distal demonstrative > proximate demonstrative > NP > stressed pronoun > unstressed pronoun > cliticized pronoun > zero.

For cases such as our text (1), Ariel convincingly showed that zero anaphora and unstressed pronouns co-occur with high accessibility of referents, whereas stressed pronouns and full lexical nouns signal low accessibility. This co-occurrence can easily be understood in terms of cognitive processes of activation: High accessibility markers signal the *default* choice of continued activation of the current topical referent. Low accessibility anaphoric devices such as full NPs or indefinite articles signal the terminated activation of the current topical referent, and the activation of another topic. Ariel (1990) even argued that binding conditions on the distribution and interpretation of pronominal and anaphoric expressions are actually the 'grammaticalized versions' of cognitive processes of attention and accessibility of concepts that are referred to linguistically. This accessibility theory is based on earlier work by Chafe and Givón: "Chafe (1976, 1994) was the first to argue for a direct connection between referential forms and cognitive status. Accessibility theory can be seen as an extension of his (and later Givón's 1983) basic insight" (Ariel, 2001, p. 60).

Many functional and cognitive linguists have argued that the grammar of referential coherence can be shown to play an important role in the mental operations of connecting incoming information to the existing mental representations. More and more empirical data from corpus studies have become available to underpin this cognitive interpretation of referential phenomena, following a route guided by functional linguists like DuBois (1980). In a distributional study, Givón (1995), for instance, showed that in English the indefinite article *a(n)* is typically used to introduce nontopical referents, whereas topical referents are introduced by *this*. In addition, there is a clear interaction between grammatical subjecthood and the demonstrative *this*: most *this*-marked NPs also appear as grammatical subjects in a sentence, whereas a majority of *a(n)*-marked NPs occurred as nonsubjects. Across languages there appears to be a topic persistence of referents: In active–transitive clauses the topic persistence of subject NPs is systematically larger than that of object NPs.

PSYCHOLINGUISTICS: THE PROCESSING OF REFERENTIAL SIGNALS

Experimental research on text and discourse processing has demonstrated the psychological reality of linguistic indicators of referential coherence. Online studies of pronominal reference have resulted in the formulation of cognitive parsing principles for anaphoric reference (e.g., Garrod & Sanford, 1994; Sanford & Garrod, 1994; see also Ariel, 2001 for a discussion of the relations between linguistic and psycholinguistic insights on these issues). For instance, it is easier to resolve a pronoun with only one possible referent, and it is easier to resolve pronouns with proximal referents than distant ones. Classical eye fixation studies have shown that anaphoric expressions are most often resolved immediately (e.g., Carpenter & Just, 1977; Ehrlich & Rayner, 1983).

(3) a. The guard mocked one of the prisoners in the machine shop.
b. He had been at the prison for only one week.

When readers came on ambiguous pronouns such as *he* in (3b), readers frequently look back in the text (i.e., make regressive eye fixations). More than 50% of these regressive fixations were to one of the two nouns in the text preceding the pronoun, suggesting that readers indeed attempt to resolve the pronoun immediately. As for the meaning representation, it has been shown that readers have difficulty understanding the text correctly when the antecedent and referent are too far apart and reference takes the form of a pronoun.

Although less research has been conducted concerning the exact working of accessibility markers as processing instructions, the influence of typical discourse phenomena like prominence of a referent in the discourse context is well-researched. Garrod and Sanford (1985) used a spelling error detection procedure, and Garrod, Freudenthal, and Boyle (1993) did an eye-tracking study based on that earlier experiment with texts like the following, which is a simplified version.

(4) A dangerous incident at the pool
Elizabeth was an inexperienced swimmer and wouldn't have gone in if the male lifeguard hadn't been standing by the pool. But as soon as she got out of her depth she started to panic and wave her hands about in a frenzy.
Target:
Within seconds she sank into the pool. (Thematic, Consistent)
Within seconds she jumped into the pool. (Thematic, Inconsistent)
Within seconds he jumped into the pool. (Nonthematic, Consistent)
Within seconds he sank into the pool. (Nonthematic, Inconsistent).
(A simplified version of experimental texts used by Garrod et al., 1993)

The eye-tracking data show strong evidence for very early detection of inconsistency, as apparent from longer fixations (in this case on the verb), but only in the case where the pronoun maintains reference to the focused thematic subject of the passage, that is, in the thematic conditions. In nonthematic conditions when the pronoun does not refer to the subject in focus, there is no evidence for early detection of inconsistency.

In recent approaches to discourse anaphora, the modeling of this type of discourse focusing is pivotal, see especially *Centering Theory* (Walker, Joshi, & Prince, 1998), which aims at modeling the center of attention in discourse in terms of the relationship of attentional state, inferential complexity and the form of referring expressions in a given discourse segment. Centering theory makes explicit predictions about the referent that is 'in focus' at a certain moment in a discourse. It is even predicted that the degree of coherence exhibited by a textual sequence is determined by the extent to which such a sequence conforms to the Centering constraints. These constraints suggest that topic continuity is the default discourse situation, because frequent topic-shifting results in less local coherence.

The precise predictions of Centering Theory not only show how linguistic expressions of referential coherence can function as processing instructions, they also suggest that there is a referential linguistic system at the discourse level, which is a challenging topic for further investigation (see Cornish, 1999).

Vonk, Hustinx, and Simons (1992) also showed the relevance of discourse context for the interpretation of referential expressions. Sometimes anaphors are more specific than would be necessary for their identificational function (i.e., full NPs are used rather than pronominal expressions). The authors convincingly argue that this phenomenon can be explained in terms of the thematic development of discourse: If a character is referred to by a proper name after a run of pronominal references, then the name itself serves to indicate that a shift in topic is occurring. Readers process the referential expressions differently, as becomes apparent from reading times.

Where anaphoric reference modulates the availability of previously mentioned concepts, cataphoric devices change the availability of concepts for the text that follows. Gernsbacher and Shroyer (1989) demonstrated the reader's sensitivity for this type of linguistic indicator of reference. They contrasted cataphoric reference by way of the indefinite *a(n)* versus the definite *this* to refer to a newly introduced referent in a story. For example, the new referent *egg* was introduced either as 'an egg' or as 'this egg'. It was hypothesized that the cataphor *this* would signal that a concept is likely to be mentioned again in the following story and that therefore the *this*-cataphor results in a higher activation. Participants listened to texts and were then asked to continue the text after the critical concept. They appeared to refer sooner and more often to a concept introduced by *this* than by *an*. These and other results show that concepts that were marked as a potential discourse topic by *this* are more strongly activated, more resistant to being suppressed in activation, as well as more effective in suppressing the activation of other concepts (Gernsbacher & Jescheniak, 1995). It is this type of finding that provides the psycholinguistic underpinning for the idea of 'grammar as a processing instructor'.

By now, the results of online studies of pronominal reference enable the formulation of cognitive parsing principles for anaphoric reference (cf. Garrod & Sanford, 1994 for an overview; also Gernsbacher, 1989; Sanford & Garrod, 1994). Person, number, and gender obviously guide pronominal resolution. More interestingly, data from reading time, eye-tracking, and priming studies show that it takes less processing cost to

- resolve pronouns with only one possible referent than several;
- resolve pronouns with proximal referents than distant ones;
- resolve reference to topical concepts than to less topical ones.

One obvious explanation for these findings is accessibility: Anaphors are instructions to connect incoming information with already mentioned referents, and the referent nodes can be more or less accessible. As a result, it takes more or less processing time to understand anaphors (Gernsbacher, 1990).

TEXT PRODUCTION

So far, we discussed the relevance of linguistic signals of accessibility as well as the dynamic process of incremental text and discourse comprehension. It is important to note that similar tendencies exist in research on production, even though there is in general less attention for production studies. Levelt (1989) suggested this is due to the bias in psycholinguistics toward perception research, at the cost of production research. Along the same lines, Kintsch, presenting an overview of discourse psychological work (1994, p. 728) remarked that "many psychological studies have concerned themselves with this problem in the past few years, although overwhelmingly with the comprehension rather than the production side."

Where empirical findings such as longer or shorter reading times of segments are taken to indicate the level of activation of a concept being processed during text understanding, the online registration of pause times opens a promising route to gain further insight into the online processes of text production. Schilperoord (1996) used the method of analyzing the location and duration of pauses during written discourse production to open up the 'black box' of a discourse producer's cognitive representation. He found that text producers tend to pause longer before segments located high in a structural hierarchy of the text under production, than before segments located low in such a hierarchy. If we assume that differences in pause time reflect differences in cognitive effort needed to retrieve mental representations, then it can be hypothesized that the hierarchical structure of discourse is a crucial factor in determining the online accessibility of information (Schilperoord & Sanders, 1997, 1999). This line of work, in which a cognitively inspired text-analysis (Sanders & van Wijk, 1996) is combined with online psycholinguistic research methods, is another example of how the combination of linguistic and psycholinguistic methods contributes to the development of integrated theories of language structure and language processes.

Accessibility and Coherence in this Issue

The overview we have presented so far has shown how accessibility is one of the most important challenges at the intersection of linguistic and psycholinguistic studies of text and discourse processing. There is a logical division of labor: (text and discourse) linguists identify the relevant signals that guide the interpretation, develop theories on how the linguistic realization of information systematically varies as to 'instruct' the interpreters, and—ideally—check the validity of their theoretical work in natural language corpora. Psycholinguists develop cognitive theories on how the actual processing occurs and test these theories in psycholinguistic experiments.

This sketch of an interdisciplinary field in which this division of labor and the interaction about the results actually take place may sound idealistic. Still, we think that this special issue shows it really exists. We have been lucky enough to get a group of prominent researchers together[1], who are important representatives of their line of work in the study of accessibility, from linguistic and psycholinguistic study, and in the latter case from interpretation as well as production. These five articles show how accessibility phenomena need to be studied from a linguistic and a psycholinguistic angle.

Ariel discusses the linguistic means of reference to discourse entities, and in doing so distinguishes between discourse profiles and discourse functions. Elaborating on her Accessibility theory, she formulates three hypotheses she encourages psycholinguists to test.

Linderholm, Virtue, Tzeng, and van den Broek discuss a typically psychological framework to model allocation of attention in their *Landscape Model of Reading*. The model addresses how various text characteristics (linguistic, discourse-structural) guide the reader's attention during reading and how they affect the mental representations readers construct. The referential forms discussed earlier are one of these textual devices determining the workings of the model, which is claimed to be an adequate model of the online reading process. This article once again underscores the importance of the notion of 'activation' as an explanatory concept in understanding the reading process and its result: a coherent mental representation of the information expressed in the text.

Gernsbacher, Robertson, Palladino, and Werner use Gernsbacher's *Structure Building Framework* to explain new experimental data about readers' mental representations during narrative comprehension. They specifically investigated whether readers' access to their mental representations of the main character in a narrative becomes enhanced (producing a "benefit") when the character is rementioned, and whether readers' access to the main character in a narrative becomes weakened or interfered with (producing a "cost") when a new character is introduced. Readers demonstrated increased accessibility to the main character when it was rementioned in the narrative, and readers demonstrated reduced accessibility to the main character when a new character was introduced. Their work suggests that successful narrative comprehension involves managing mental representa-

---

[1]Most articles in this special issue are based on papers presented at the International workshop on text representation: Linguistic and psycholinguistics aspects, held at Utrecht University in July 1997.

tions of salient and often times interfering characters. This study is a convincing example of a dynamic processing theory of accessibility in discourse.

Then we move to discourse production. Maes, Arts, and Noordman investigate the effect of two language-in-use factors on the introduction and maintenance of referents in instructive discourse. These factors, which were implemented as conditions in an instructive production task, were the assumed visual identity for the reader of the objects or referents to be referred to in instructions (*visually same* vs. *visually different*) and the assumed goal of the reader (*reading to do* vs. *reading to learn*). The results show that both factors have a strong impact on the writers' referential behavior. *Visually same* referents are introduced and reintroduced fairly systematically by means of perceptually overspecified NPs. *Visually different* referents are introduced systematically by extra propositional identification speech acts and they are reintroduced more often by attenuated anaphoric expressions. Apart from that, writers show a number of referential strategies which fit with the assumed reader's goal. Writers in the *reading to learn* condition use more overspecified expressions than writers in the *reading to do* condition.

The results of the study by Maes and colleagues are important, not only because they concern production, but also because they give rise to an extension of accessibility and other theories that account for the form of referential expressions. Their results suggest that referential expressions that are more informative than necessary for identification purposes do not only occur when the activation level of discourse referents is low, but also when the writer anticipates specific conditions in which the information will be used by the reader. This shows how an adequate account of accessibility should not only include the linguistic and psycholinguistic aspects discussed here, but also *functional* aspects like the writers' and readers' communicative goals. For instance, when writers assume readers to be very precise processors of the textual information because they use the text as an instruction, they will use a different referential strategy than when readers are expected to process the information as 'just' an informative or narrative text.

Together, these contributions augment our growing knowledge of accessibility in text and discourse processing. These contributions illuminate how accessibility is marked in a text or a discourse; how readers and listeners respond to those markings; how mental representations evolve and change as a direct result of accessibility. These contributions epitomize one strength of the journal, *Discourse Processes:* its interdisciplinary welcome and offerings. It is our hope as editors of this special issue that the text we have amassed will affect the journal's readers' representations in just the ways that we as linguists and psycholinguists theorize as beneficial.

REFERENCES

Ariel, M. (1990). *Accessing noun-phrase antecedents.* London: Routledge.

Ariel, M. (2001). Accessibility theory: An overview. In T. Sanders, J. Schilperoord, & W. Spooren (Eds.), *Text representation: Linguistic and psycholinguistic aspects* (pp. 29–87). Amsterdam: Benjamins.

Carpenter, P. A., & Just, M. A. (1977). Reading comprehension as eyes see it. In M. Just & P. Carpenter (Eds.), *Cognitive processes in comprehension* (pp. 109–139). Hillsdale, NJ: Lawrence Erlbaum Associates, Inc.

Chafe, W. L. (1976). Givenness, contrastiveness, definiteness, subjects, topics and point of view. In C. N. Li (Ed.), *Subject and topic* (pp. 25–55). New York: Academic.

Chafe, W. L. (1994). *Discourse, consciousness, and time. The flow and displacement of conscious experience in speaking and writing.* Chicago: Chicago University Press.

Cornish, F. (1999). *Anaphora, discourse and understanding. Evidence from English and French.* New York: Oxford University Press.

DuBois, J. W. (1980). Beyond definiteness: The trace of identity in discourse. In W. L. Chafe, (Ed.), *The Pear Stories: Cognitive, cultural and linguistic aspects of narrative production* (pp. 203–274). Norwood, NJ: Ablex.

Ehrlich, K., & Rayner, K. (1983). Pronoun assignment and semantic integration during reading: Eye movements and immediacy of processing. *Journal of Verbal Learning and Verbal Behavior, 22,* 75–87.

Gaddy, M. L., van den Broek, P., & Sung, Y. (2001). The influence of text cues on the allocation of attention during reading. In T. Sanders, J. Schilperoord, & W. Spooren (Eds.), *Text representation: Linguistic and psycholinguistic aspects* (pp. 89–110). Amsterdam: Benjamins.

Garrod, S. C., Freudenthal, D., & Boyle, E. (1993). The role of different types of anaphor in the on-line resolution of sentences in a discourse. *Journal of Memory and Language, 32,* 1–30.

Garrod, S. C., & Sanford, A. J. (1985). On the real-time character of interpretation during reading. *Language and Cognitive Processes, 1,* 43–61.

Garrod, S. C., & Sanford, A. J. (1994). Resolving sentences in a discourse context: How discourse representation affects language understanding. In M. A. Gernsbacher (Ed.), *Handbook of psycholinguistics* (pp. 675–698). San Diego, CA: Academic.

Gernsbacher, M. A. (1989). Mechanisms that improve referential access. *Cognition, 32,* 99–156.

Gernsbacher, M. A. (1990). *Language comprehension as structure building.* Hillsdale, NJ: Lawrence Erlbaum Associates, Inc.

Gernsbacher, M. A., & Givón, T. (1995). (Eds.). *Coherence in spontaneous text.* Amsterdam: Benjamins.

Gernsbacher, M. A., & Jescheniak, J. (1995). Cataphoric devices in spoken discourse. *Cognitive Psychology, 29,* 24–58.

Gernsbacher, M. A., & Shroyer, S. (1989). The cataphoric use of the indefinite *this* in spoken narratives. *Memory & Cognition, 17,* 536–540.

Givón, T. (1983). (Ed.). *Topic continuity in discourse: A quantitative crosslanguage study.* Amsterdam: Benjamins.

Givón, T. (1995). Coherence in text vs. coherence in mind. In M. A. Gernsbacher & T. Givón (Eds.), *Coherence in spontaneous text* (pp. 59–115). Amsterdam: Benjamins. Typological Studies in Language, 31.

Graesser, A. C., Millis, K. K., & Zwaan, R. (1997). Discourse comprehension. *Annual Review of Psychology, 48,* 163–189.

Kintsch, W. (1994). The psychology of discourse processing. In M. A. Gernsbacher (ed.), *Handbook of Psycholinguistics.* (pp. 721–739). San Diego, CA: Academic.

Kintsch, W. (1998). *Comprehension. A paradigm for cognition.* New York: Cambridge University Press.

Levelt, W. J. M. (1989). *Speaking. From intention to articulation.* Cambridge, MA: Bradford/MIT Press.

Matthews, P. (1994). *The Guinness book of records 1994.* New York: Bantam Books.

Sanders, T., & Spooren, W. (2001). Text representation as an interface between language and its users. In T. Sanders, J. Schilperoord, & W. Spooren (Eds.), *Text representation: Linguistic and psycholinguistic aspects* (pp. 1–25). Amsterdam: Benjamins.

Sanders, T., & Spooren, W. (2002). Discourse and text structure. In D. Geeraerts & H. Cuykens (Eds.), *Handbook of Cognitive Linguistic.* Oxford, England: Clarendon.

Sanders, T., & van Wijk, C. (1996). PISA–A procedure for analyzing the structure of explanatory texts. *Text, 16,* 91–132.

Sanford, A. J., & Garrod, S. C. (1994). Selective processes in text understanding. In M. A. Gernsbacher, (Ed.), *Handbook of Psycholinguistics* (pp. 699–720). San Diego, CA: Academic.

Schilperoord, J. (1996). *It's about time. Temporal aspects of cognitive processes in text production.* Amsterdam: Rodopi.

Schilperoord, J., & Sanders, T. (1997). Pauses, cognitive rhythms and discourse structure. An empirical study of discourse production. In A. Liebert, G. Redeker, & L. Waugh (Eds.), *Disourse and Perspective in Cognitive Linguistics.* (pp. 247–249). Amsterdam: Benjamins.

Schilperoord, J., & Sanders, T. (1999). How hierarchical structure affects retrieval processes; Implications of pause and text analysis. In D. Galbraith, & M. Torrance (Eds.), *Conceptual processes in writing.* (pp. 13–30). Amsterdam: Amsterdam University Press.

van den Broek, P., Young, M., Tzeng, Y., & Linderholm, T. (1998). The landscape model of reading: Inferences and the on-line construction of a memory representation. In H. Van Oostendorp & S. R. Goldman (Eds.), *The construction of mental representations during reading* (pp. 71–98). Mahwah, NJ: Lawrence Erlbaum Associates, Inc.

Vonk, W., Hustinx, L. G. M. M., & Simons, W. H. G. (1992). The use of referential expressions in structuring discourse. *Language and Cognitive Processes, 7,* 301–333.

Walker, M. A., Joshi, A., & Prince, E. (Eds.). (1998). *Centering Theory in discourse.* Oxford, England: Clarendon.

DISCOURSE PROCESSES, *37*(2), 91–116

Accessibility Marking: Discourse Functions, Discourse Profiles, and Processing Cues

Mira Ariel
Department of Linguistics
Tel Aviv University

When accounting for the usage of some linguistic form, one can refer to its discourse profile, all concomitant features frequently co-occurring with that form in discourse, or abstract a more general claim about its discourse function, referring only to the necessary and sufficient conditions for the proper occurrence of the form. This article discusses discourse profile and discourse function approaches to referring expressions in linguistic and psycholinguistic research. Focusing on English prenominal possessive noun phrases (NPs, e.g., *my career*), I argue that although their (prototypical) discourse profile is amenable to clearly defined automatic processing or production cues, and to explaining potential grammaticizations, only their discourse functions can account for all the forms actually attested in discourse. I conclude that both types of accounts are linguistically relevant, and I propose that psycholinguists devise experiments to test the three hypotheses outlined (discourse profiles, discourse functions, and a combination of discourse profiles and discourse functions).

REFERRING EXPRESSIONS, DISCOURSE PROFILES, AND DISCOURSE FUNCTIONS

Discourse Profiles and Discourse Functions

When language users follow a consistent linguistic pattern, what is it exactly that governs their behavior? What knowledge should the linguist attribute to the native speaker? When stating the principle governing this behavior, should we adhere as

Correspondence and requests for reprints should be sent to Mira Ariel, Department of Linguistics, Tel Aviv University, Tel Aviv, Israel, 69978. E-mail: mariel@post.tau.ac.il much as possible to the actual findings, or should we abstract away from the detailed findings and offer a general principle? If so, how general? *Discourse profiles* are relatively concrete, low-level generalizations about the conditions of use and interpretations of linguistic forms in actual discourse. They describe all the features frequently co-occurring with the expression. Crucially, however, not all these features are obligatory. *Discourse functions*, on the other hand, are higher-level generalizations, abstracted away from various discourse profiles, each compatible with a few discourse profiles. These include all and only those features that obligatorily co-occur with the form. Do language users store highly abstract principles of language use (discourse functions), or do they actually rely on low-level, more concrete generalizations (discourse profiles) when selecting or interpreting specific linguistic expressions? Psycholinguists face similar questions when interpreting experimental results. What should they attribute to the language user? The very concrete variables tested for, or more abstract generalizations?

This article addresses this question with respect to referring expressions. Should these be accounted for by reference to discourse functions or to discourse profiles? Accessibility Theory (Ariel, 1988b, 1990, 2001) was offered as a theory about the discourse functions of referring expressions. Under Accessibility Theory, each referring expression is seen as coding a specific degree of mental accessibility as its discourse function, which means that its use is restricted to just this function, even though it may manifest a variety of discourse profiles. A specific example I will discuss in more detail are English prenominal possessive NPs (e.g., *my career*). The main body of data used in this research is a slightly edited first person narrative from Morris (1994, pp. 129–139), which contains 133 possessive NPs. Additional data were drawn from the Corpus of Spoken American English (Du Bois, 2000).

The question of discourse profiles versus discourse functions is definitely not restricted to the use and interpretation of possessive NPs. The next section briefly summarizes previous analyses of other referring expressions (pronouns and definite descriptions) in terms of either discourse profiles or discourse functions. In the following section, I will first argue that an appropriate account of the referring expressions occurring in possessive NPs must be in terms of their generalized or abstract discourse functions, rather than their prototypical discourse profiles. I will argue that the discourse function(s) of different types of possessive NPs are just like those of any referring expression, namely, they should properly code the degree of mental accessibility associated with the entity referred to. Nonetheless, in view of the crucial role played by prototypical discourse profiles in linguistic change and of similar low-level generalizations in language production or processing, I will suggest (in the final section) that the native speaker competence probably encompasses both the discourse functions and the discourse profiles associated with linguistic forms. I end with a plea for psycholinguists to explore what are psychologically real representations of linguistic patterns: the most general and abstract discourse functions, a set of prototypical discourse profiles, or some combination of the two alternatives.

Discourse Profile and Discourse Function Accounts of Pronouns and Definite Descriptions

Previous analyses of pronouns and definite descriptions can illustrate the differences between discourse function and discourse profile accounts for referring expressions. For example, a repeated finding in the literature is that main characters in narratives are referred to by pronouns, whereas subsidiary ones are referred to by definite descriptions. How is the linguist to formulate the discourse pattern identified? Karmiloff-Smith (1985) chose to characterize the usage of pronouns and definite descriptions in just these terms, according to what I would term their discourse profiles. According to her, referring expressions are selected according to their discourse roles: Pronouns refer to main characters, whereas definite descriptions refer to subsidiary characters. According to Accessibility Theory, however, these discourse profiles are merely manifestations of more abstract discourse functions. Pronouns tend to refer to main characters in narratives just because main characters are highly accessible and it is the discourse function of pronouns to refer to highly accessible discourse entities. Definite descriptions, on the other hand, are said to code a low degree of accessibility as their discourse function, and should be used when the speaker assesses that the mental representation of the intended entity is only entertained at a low degree of accessibility. Subsidiary characters often meet this condition, and hence are coded by definite descriptions. This is why we can discern a recurrent discourse profile for definite descriptions whereby they refer to subsidiary characters.

In fact, however, it is not always an easy matter to draw a distinction between conditions that are only part of the prototypical discourse profile and conditions obligatorily placed as discourse functions.[1] Discourse functions too are often based on empirical findings, which, although statistically very significant, rarely amount to 100% of the cases. If so, how can one tell if the identified variables (e.g., main vs. subsidiary characters) constitute a necessary aspect of the discourse function of some accessibility marker, or merely frequent but nonobligatory aspects of its occurrence, for instance, part of its prototypical discourse profile? To make things worse, in arguing for a particular discourse function, linguists perforce rely on empirical results for particular discourse profiles. For instance, to argue that definite descriptions code a low degree of accessibility (as their discourse function), I have cited findings regarding their discourse profiles. Thus, anaphoric defi-

[1]But see Prince (1992) for a clear distinction between prototypical, canonical subjects—marked definite—and the category of subjects, which cannot be said to require definiteness, because not all participants are definite.

nite descriptions refer to an entity not immediately available in the current text in 83.1% of the cases (see Ariel, 1990). These are divided somewhat unequally between cases where the entities retrieved are mentioned in the same paragraph, but not in the current or the previous sentence (55.1%) and cases where the entities retrieved are mentioned in previous paragraph(s) (44.9%).[2] I have thus shown a correlation between a linguistic form (definite descriptions) and two contexts: (a) within the paragraph but not adjacent and (b) across a paragraph boundary. Do these contexts provide evidence for one abstract discourse function, or do they constitute two discourse profiles for definite descriptions? If it is one discourse function, is it some concept of cognitive distance, or is it the even more general concept of low accessibility?

Actually, by referring to the two previous contexts (as well as others), my intention was to exemplify the higher generalization about a single discourse function–namely, that definite descriptions require the intended referents to be entertained at a relatively low degree of accessibility. I did not wish to argue that definite descriptions are accounted for directly by reference to these (and other) *prototypical discourse profiles* per se. Such a reading of my claims substitutes prototypical discourse profiles (various contexts of conceptually long distance) for the discourse function (a low degree of accessibility). Indeed, (Psycho)linguists have sometimes taken prototypical discourse profiles for discourse functions (see Maes & Noordman's interpretation of Accessibility Theory, 1995). Even though I have argued that referring expressions each code a specific discourse function, regardless of their prototypical discourse profile(s), it is, in fact, possible that speakers and addressees rely directly on concrete contextual factors when selecting or interpreting referring expressions.

Indeed, Fox (1987) adopted the discourse profile approach for referring expressions. Fox restricted her examination to third person singular human anaphoric references performed by pronouns and lexical NPs, justifying her choice as follows: "I have narrowed the domain in this way to look at anaphora in its *prototypical use*: tracking a participant through a discourse" (p. 2, emphasis added). She then switches from a description of what she terms the prototypical use of discourse anaphora to the prototypical uses of pronouns and definite descriptions as anaphoric devices.[3] Note that focusing on discourse profiles tends to highlight differ-

---

[2]I view these contexts as constituting potentially two separate profiles because across the paragraph boundary, no restriction is placed on the distance between the last mention and the current mention of the referent.

[3]Note that although it may be true that prototypically, discourse anaphoric expressions in general track humans, this is not necessarily true of each anaphoric device. Specifically, anaphoric definite descriptions most probably do not refer to humans prototypically. In the personal narrative analyzed here, the anaphoric definite descriptions referred to humans only in a third of the cases (62, 33.2%). In fact, even the majority of those I counted as human are actually references to the sets of people associated with certain institutions (e.g., *the university*, see Note 5), and are then not singular in reference, as the prototype is assumed to be by Fox.

ences between uses, and may therefore eclipse commonalties between them (cf. the discourse profiles of subsidiary character, some distance within the paragraph and across paragraphs with the one discourse function of low accessibility for definite descriptions). Indeed, Fox ends up concluding that each genre has its distinct referential style of definite descriptions and pronouns, because of the different discourse profiles pronouns and lexical NPs have in different genres (see also Jucker, 1996; Lord & Dahlgren, 1997). Toole (1996), Ariel (2002), and Ariel (in press) argued that distinct genre profiles of referring expressions do not necessarily amount to distinct genre discourse functions.

Dahl and Fraurud (1996) and Fraurud's (1996) analysis of animacy of referential forms shows the problematicity of generalizing from a prototypical discourse profile to a discourse function. In their Swedish data, pronouns retrieved some human, but no nonhuman antecedents that were not mentioned in the immediately preceding sentence. All the nonhuman referents coded by pronouns had a nearby antecedent. Now, is this a discourse profile, or a grammatical discourse function? Should we say that pronouns cannot refer to nonadjacent nonhuman antecedents? It seems that this is true in 100% of the cases, after all. However, it is quite possible that we need not impose a grammatical discourse function in this case. Fraurud's findings can be seen as reflecting the discourse profile of pronouns with nonhuman antecedents: Nonhuman entities are not as salient to us as humans are. If so, we should only expect that nonhumans in the same distance as human antecedents are entertained at a lower degree of accessibility. Hence the inability of pronouns (high accessibility markers) to refer to them. To distinguish between these two options we should examine cases where nonhumans are very salient, as when they are the continuing discourse topics. If they cannot be referred to by nonimmediate pronouns even in such cases, then Fraurud's findings do not merely constitute a recurrent discourse profile. Rather, they constitute a grammaticized discourse function.[4]

In general, artificial intelligence researchers have tended to adopt some version of the discourse profile approach, but they do not restrict themselves to one prototypical discourse profile per form. They may list an ordered set of simple "practical" interpretative strategies, which are specific instances of the general abstraction (e.g., Hobbs, 1976; Rumelhart & Levin, 1975). This "list of discourse profiles" approach is understandable in view of AI researchers' interest in automatic computerized procedures, which cannot be defined over abstractions such as high or low degrees of accessibility. It is then reasonable to concentrate on concretely defined low-level generalizations when results are robust enough. Indeed, it is impressive that a computer program can correctly identify the intended antecedent for a pronoun in 90% of the cases by assuming a few discourse profiles for

[4]Of interest, Chappell (1996) noted that the possessors in double subject constructions in the Chinese narration of the Pear Story were always the human protagonists, never any props, even though the latter could have topical role.

it. Provided there is a gender and number match, in the program by Norman and colleagues (1975), a pronoun refers to an entity either previously referred to by a pronoun, or it is the grammatical subject of the previous clause. If unsuccessful, this procedure may be repeated for a preceding clause. Does this program testify to the actual human strategies employed, or are these merely operational strategies based on the higher discourse function of high accessibility, which is the one relied on by language users?

Psycholinguists too have sought to establish concrete, low-level interpretative *strategies*, even cues, or heuristic devices, rather than highly abstract and general discourse functions (see e.g., Armstrong et al., 1983; Bates & MacWhinney, 1989; Ehrlich, 1980; Maes, 1996; Maes & Noordman, 1995; McDonald & MacWhinney, 1995; Sanford & Garrod, 1981). Is the discourse profile(s) approach justified? Is it sufficient? Must speakers have access to a more general (discourse function) formulation of use conditions instead? Or, do both representations play a role in language use? Based on linguistic findings for prenominal possessive NPs, I will tentatively conclude that the dual "redundant" approach is the correct answer. I will then suggest that psycholinguists devise experiments to test the competing accounts of discourse functions and discourse profiles for how speakers actually process (and produce) linguistic expressions.

ENGLISH PRENOMINAL POSSESSIVE NPS AS EXAMPLE: DISCOURSE PROFILE AND DISCOURSE FUNCTION

Prenominal possessive NPs refer to two discourse entities between which some asymmetric relation obtains. This relation can be of possession, but most often it is not. Instead, some association between the entities is contextually inferred (see Chappell & Thompson, 1992 for Chinese). Note the following, where the association between the husband and the terrorist is that the latter killed the former:

1. Tell Mrs. Osher that I will not release *her husband's terrorist* (originally, Hebrew, Prime Minister Rabin, as quoted in *Haaretz* 5.5.1993).

According to Langacker (1991, p. 170) and Taylor (1994, 1996), the relationship between the anchor (the "possessor") and the anchored (the "possessee") is that the anchor provides a reference point for the anchored. The anchor must provide a valid cue for accessing the anchored. This is potentially a discourse function for prenominal possessive NPs, which would dictate the information status coded by the two NPs comprising the possessive NP. As the data will show, however, this is merely a prototypical discourse profile of possessive NPs. The next two sections analyze in turn the prototypical discourse profile and the discourse functions of the NPs in English prenominal possessive NPs. I show that characterizing possessive

NPs according to their prototypical discourse profile accounts for only the majority of their occurrences (between 65% and 100% of the cases). However, characterizing them according to the discourse functions of the anchor and the anchored NPs enables us to generalize over (virtually) 100% of their occurrences.

The Prototypical Discourse Profile of English Prenominal Possessive NPs

The following is a prototypical example of a prenominal possessive NP in my data (unless otherwise specified, all examples are quoted from Morris, 1994, and I indicate in parentheses the page number and the number I assigned the specific example in my data):

2. And the stress and rumors had damaged *my psyche* and *my ability to function* (pp. 134, 143–144).

The data summarized in Table 1 show that the referent of the anchor, as *my* in (2) is invariably human. Humans also constitute 77% of the anchors in Taylor's (1996) data (see also Chappell & Thompson, 1992).[5] It is very often singular (compare with Taylor's 84%). In studies limited to human anchors (and anchoreds), we found a preference for men over women in the role of anchors in nonfeminist writings, but not so in more egalitarian writings (see Ariel, 1988a; Ariel & Giora, 1998). For the most part, the anchor also represents Given/accessible information, in fact already referred to in the same paragraph. Only three examples had a brand new anchor (Taylor had 6%). I had gotten similar results in Ariel (1996), where I examined Hebrew newspaper editorials: All of the Hebrew anchors were locally previously mentioned.[6] The anchor also tends to be globally salient in the discourse: Many were mentioned at least 10 times in the narrative (see also Brown, 1983). Predictably, therefore, the prototypical anchor is coded by a pronoun (75% in Taylor's data). Pronouns refer to highly accessible entities (see Ariel, 1990; Chafe, 1976; Givón, 1983a; Sanford & Garrod, 1981, inter alia).

The prototypical anchored entity is the mirror image of the anchor (see Table 2). It refers to a nonhuman (see also Brown, 1983). In studies restricted to human anchoreds, more women than men occur in nonfeminist writings (Ariel, 1988a; Ariel & Giora, 1998). Anchoreds tend to represent new information (i.e., they are first-mentions, see also Brown, 1983; Chappell & Thompson, 1992; Givón, 1983a). These new entities are, however, relatively easily inferable based

[5]I treat entities such as The University of Iowa as human, because the institution is portrayed as acting intentionally. Taylor did not count such NPs as human, which accounts for some of the difference in our numbers.

[6]Hebrew, however, does not distinguish between pre- and postnominal possessive NPs.

TABLE 1
Statistical Properties of the Anchor

Property	*Number of Instances*	*Percentage*
Human	133	100
Singular	110	82.7
Mentioned in the same paragraph	116	87.2
Brand new	3	2.25
Globally salient	87	65.4
Coded by pronoun	121	90.1

on their anchor. Addressees rely on general stereotypic assumptions (e.g., people have opinions, families, friends, and body parts, hence, *their skin* 129: 18; *Her credentials* 133: 100), or on assumptions appropriate for the specific discourse (academics have careers, promotions, hence, *my promotion to full professor* 133:118). No wonder it is coded by a lexical NP: Definite lexical NPs are used for entities that are accessible, but at a relatively low degree of accessibility. The anchored is the head noun in possessive NPs. Its newness or nonsaliency is then compatible with the finding that possessive NPs tend to be coded as nonsubjects (87% in Brown's, 1983 data). The anchored NP does not constitute a globally salient entity in the discourse (i.e., at most, it is mentioned once or twice again in the narrative). It is not even locally prominent. Hardly ever is it referred to again in definite form without the same anchor in the same paragraph (see also Brown, 1983, but see Givón, 1983a for different results).

Table 2 summarizes the findings for anchored NPs.

Thus, it seems that the prototypical possessive NP is a nonsubject that introduces a new but inferable, transient, and relatively noncentral discourse entity (i.e., inanimate, women for non-egalitarians) by anchoring it to a highly accessible, prominent, human (preferably a man for non-egalitarians) discourse entity (see Hawkins, 1981 & Deane, 1987, 1992 for "topicality" hierarchies of anchors and anchoreds, whereby the anchor must be higher on the hierarchy than the an-

TABLE 2
Statistical Properties of the Anchored

Property	*Number of Instances*	*Percentage*
Nonhuman	96	72.2
First mention inferable	90	67.7
Coded by lexical NP	133	100
Nonsubject	86	64.7
Not globally salient	116	87.2
Referred to again in the same paragraph	5	3.8

chored). As Taylor (1996) noted, prenominal possessives almost invariably refer to specific, usually also definite referents.

Note that although most of the previous findings do not reach categoriality (100%), aspects of prototypical discourse profiles may have grammatical repercussions nonetheless. Lehmann (1985) suggested that semantic affinities explain the identity in form between ergatives (NPs coding semantic agents) and possessors in many languages (see also Blake, 1994). Du Bois (1988) suggested that it is the similarity between the *discourse profiles* of anchors or possessors and ergatives—both are prototypically human, Given and coded nonlexically—which explains this marking system, despite the fact that possessors are not the agents in their clauses (see also Duranti & Ochs, 1990 for such affinities). We could similarly propose that the similarity between the discourse profiles of grammatical patients (direct objects) and anchored entities (both are predominantly nonhuman) motivates the assignment of the same case to both in some languages (see Blake, 1994). Heine (1997) noted that possessors consistently precede their possessees. This is highly compatible with the anchoring function of the possessor (Heine referred to it as the topic).

The prototypical discourse profile of possessive NPs can then become partially grammaticized in a number of ways (additional examples are presented in Ariel, 2002). Because grammaticizations must happen in real discourse time, we must assume that speakers are operating with low-level form-function correlations, even though they are redundant and only optional in the early stages. But are we justified in characterizing all prenominal possessive NPs in all languages by reference to their prototypical occurrences (in case these are universal)? In the following, I will suggest that such an account, although motivated, is insufficient by itself.

Identifying the Discourse Functions of the NPs in Prenominal Possessive NPs

In this section, I will suggest that if we correctly identify the discourse functions imposed on each of the NP forms used in possessive NPs, one generalization can account for both the prototypical and the nonprototypical cases. All the NPs in possessive NPs (anchors and anchoreds alike) are selected in accordance with Accessibility Theory (Ariel, 1985, 1988b, 1990, 2001).

According to Accessibility Theory, speakers direct their addressees' retrieval of the intended referents by signaling to them how accessible those mental entities are. Referring expressions each code a different and specific degree of mental accessibility, and the form is selected accordingly. We can tap degree of accessibility by reference to many variables, the ones relevant for the discussion at hand are topicality, distance, and competition. Mental entities corresponding to discourse topics are highly accessible. So are representations of entities recently mentioned (short distance) and ones that have no competing candidates.

Entities that are not topical, that were mentioned a while ago, and that have to compete with other candidates on the role of antecedent, are entertained at a lower degree of accessibility. The form-function correlation between referring expressions and degree of accessibility is highly motivated. Informative, rigid (roughly, uniquely referring), and phonologically prominent (long, or stressed) referring expressions code lower degrees of accessibility, while uninformative, nonrigid, and phonologically attenuated forms code a higher degree of accessibility. For the purposes of this article, it is enough to distinguish between definite lexical NPs and pronouns. The former are relatively more informative, rigid, and phonologically prominent than the latter. Hence they code a lower degree of accessibility.

It is clear that the prototypical cases abide by Accessibility Theory. If the anchors are human and have close-by antecedents (in the same paragraph), then a high accessibility marker (a pronoun) is called for. And if the anchored NP presents a first mention entity even if easily inferable, then a low accessibility marker (a definite lexical NP) is called for. The crucial point is that when we next examine the nonprototypical cases, it will become evident that although these are indeed nonprototypical in that they are not so common, they obey Accessibility Theory predictions just as prototypical cases do. We start with the nonprototypical anchors. Although usually pronominal, the anchor was not coded by a pronoun in 12 cases. These constitute only 9% of the data, but crucially, they are perfectly grammatical and discourse appropriate. Here is one example:

3. They sent me to the academic vice-president, a man named Leffler, who saw that whenever anybody in the medical school had had a grievance, the strategy had been to attack Dr Williams's character… (134: 130).

The reason Dr. Williams is referred to by a lexical NP is that he has not been mentioned in this paragraph (although he is a prominent discourse entity in the narrative). Entities of a relatively lower degree of accessibility require fuller referential forms. The more prominent antecedent in this context is Leffler, and there would also be another potentially competing antecedent for *his* (i.e., *anybody in the medical school*). Hence, the avoidance of a pronominal form for Williams. Indeed, in 7 of the 12 cases of lexical anchors, the antecedent did not occur in the current paragraph. In 2 or the 12 cases, the antecedent did occur in the same paragraph, but so was a competing antecedent. In 1 of the 12 cases, the anchor was new, although inferred. These are all circumstances enabling only a relatively lower degree of accessibility for the entity referred to. Finally, in 2 of the 12 cases, the anchor was a generic, new entity (see 5a following). These were coded by indefinite NPs. A low degree of accessibility or lack of it calls for the use of a lexical NP, rather than a pronoun.

Next, recall that reference points are often singular, and this is why the majority of the anchors are singular. Still, more than 17% are plural (see Table 1). Yet, they are as good as reference points as the singular entities are in a narrative of "we" against "them":

4. One of our expert witnesses said that… (138: 327).

Last, the possessor does not always provide a specific reference point via which a specific anchored entity is retrieved. In such cases, the anchor may be new, nonspecific or unidentifiable, and it is appropriately coded by an indefinite NP:

5. a. When someone's personal and professional reputation has been besmirched… (138: 326a).
   b. JIM: …there may be (H)…a hundred thousand dollars in there,
      which may represent…three people's,
      or four people's purchases, (Du Bois, 2000: BANK).

Nine possessive NPs (12.9%) of the 70 lexical possessor possessive NPs in 10 naturally occurring American English conversations (Du Bois, 2000) contained an indefinite possessor. In all of them the possessor does not actually serve as a reference point, and in most of them (8/9) the relation between the possessor and the head is that of possession, as in (b). Thus, Langacker's (see also Taylor, 1996) account of possessive NPs as reference points for anchored entities is restricted to the prototypical cases only.

One can still defend the discourse profile approach by redefining the relevant expression as a possessive NP with a pronominal anchor. Yet, this move does not eliminate other perfectly grammatical "exceptions" to the prototypical case. Thus, although most pronominal anchors have already been mentioned in this paragraph, 6 of the pronominal anchors (5%) have their antecedents outside the paragraph. Not surprisingly, these antecedents are highly prominent in the narrative (the narrator and the University of Iowa). Thus, if we ignore the statistically frequent context (previous mention in the same paragraph), even though it constitutes the prototypical discourse profile of the pronominal anchor (95%), and instead characterize its discourse function as marking high accessibility, we can uniformly characterize all the uses of pronominal anchors. All pronominally coded anchors are entertained at a high degree of mental accessibility, even though the source of their high accessibility varies. Some (39, 32.2%) gain their high accessibility status merely due to a previous mention in the same paragraph. These anchors are themselves transient discourse entities (and thus diverge from the prototypical profile of the anchor being a prominent discourse entity).Very few anchors gain high accessibility due only to their overall prominence in the narrative (6, 5%). Most achieve high accessibility based on both criteria (76, 62.8%).[7]

Last, although the anchors in my data were all human, the perceptive reader may have noticed a few possessive NPs with inanimate anchors in this article (e.g., *its discourse function* in the previous paragraph). Indeed, although we normally maintain humans at relatively higher degrees of accessibility than inanimates, for this article, linguistic expressions, discourse functions, discourse profiles, and anchors (the antecedent for the previous *its* is 'the anchor') are very central. Hence, they here serve as proper anchors (see Quirk, Leech, & Svartvik, 1972; Osselton, 1988). Moreover, in each case where *its* was used, the antecedent is available in the immediately preceding context. Concentrating on the prototypical profile of the anchor would have made these instances seem incomprehensible or unacceptable, which they are not. The Corpus of Spoken American English (Du Bois, 2000) contained quite a few nonhuman anchors (e.g., *the horse's hoof* —BLACKSMITHING) and even a few inanimates (e.g., *at LCL's office* —BANK).

In fact, once we have determined that choosing an appropriate anchor form is conditioned by the degree of mental accessibility associated with the anchoring entity, regardless of it being part of a possessive NP, we can account for both the majority cases (pronominal) and the minority of lexical anchors. The latter simply code a lower degree of accessibility, and are used when the anchors are not highly accessible. Anchors, then, are no different from other discourse entities coded by pronouns and lexical NPs. Highly accessible anchors or entities are coded by pronouns, anchors or entities entertained at a relatively low degree of accessibility are coded by definite lexical NPs.

Let us now examine the nonprototypical anchored NPs in the narrative. I will suggest that even when not new, the entities referred to are still entertained at a relatively low degree of accessibility, and hence the use of a lexical NP understood as definite. A total of 39 anchored NPs (30.2%)[8] refer to Given entities. A third (13 of the 39) are paragraph-external mentions, which retrieve entities no longer highly accessible (see Ariel, 1990, and references cited therein). Two thirds of the Given anchoreds (26 of the 39) do have an antecedent in the current paragraph. Note, however, that most of these paragraph-internal second-mention anchored NPs (18 of the 26) are not straightforwardly processible as coreferent with the previous mention. The previous mention may be quite different in content, or even in exact reference. Both Gibbs (1990) and Onishi and Murphy (1993) found that an equally accessible antecedent took longer to activate when a metaphorical rather than a lit-

---

[7]It should be noted, however, that Accessibility Theory can account for the fact that overwhelmingly, the anchor is pronominal only once a possessive case has been chosen. Accessibility Theory cannot alone account for the (grammaticized) fact that family members and inalienable possessions must be anchored by possessor NPs in most cases in English, for example.

[8]I here ignore 4 nonreferntial anchored NPs, so the 100% consists of 129 instances.

eral anaphoric expression was employed (a content difference). In 6(a), the actual antecedent is a generalization over previously mentioned propositions (a content difference, therefore). In 6(b) coreferentiality is only partial:

6. a. I liked the sciences and did well. And I had teachers in high school who encouraged me… My experience confirmed the Puritan ethic… (130: 41).
   b. I was born in this country, but my parents$_{i+j}$ were born in China. My father$_j$ … (129: 2).

Even the anchored NPs that had already been mentioned in the same paragraph in (almost) identical form (8/26) do not in fact represent highly accessible antecedents. A relatively large distance (3–8 clauses) separates the two mentions, and in addition, competing potential antecedents lower the accessibility with which the antecedent is available to the addressee. The following remention of the narrator's parents as *my parents* (rather than as *they)* is typical:

7. Many of my parents$_i$' Chinese friends$_j$ would tell them$_i$ it was a waste to spend money to educate a daughter because you wanted her to get married and have children$_k$. They$_j$'d say that if girls$_l$ got too educated, it would be harder for them$_l$ to find husbands$_m$. My parents$_i$ didn't buy into that… (130: 35).

Thus, all 39 Given anchoreds are entities entertained at a relatively low degree of accessibility, justifying the use of a (definite) lexical NP.

Another feature of the prototype is the nonhumanness and nonprominence of the anchored NPs. However, over a quarter of the anchored NPs do refer to humans (see Table 2), and moreover, a few of them are referred to several times (six entities). These are then relatively prominent (e.g., the narrator's lawyer). In fact, as previously mentioned, Givón (1983a) found a high persistence for anchored entities. Taylor (1996) believed that this is due to a high number of kinship possessives with human anchoreds in Givón's data. Indeed, all persisting anchoreds in my data were human. We cannot therefore maintain the prototype of anchored NPs (new, nonhuman, nonsalient entities) as part of the generalization about their discourse function(s). Rather, because inanimates make poor topics and because anchoreds are often inanimate, it is very often the case that anchoreds do not become later topics. Yet, it is not a feature of the NP in the construction per se.

In conclusion, if we were to insist on listing a set of discourse profiles for possessive NPs, then probably the following would characterize (but not exhaust) the main profiles that possessive NPs take in actual discourse:

8. a. Possessive NPs introduce a low accessibility, inferable, transient inanimate entity by relating it to a highly accessible human discourse entity (this is the prototypical discourse profile, with a pronominal anchor, a lexical anchored, and nonsubject status).
   b. Same as (a), but the anchor is nonhuman.

c. Same as (a), but the anchor is of a lower degree of accessibility (with a lexical anchor).
d. Same as (a), but the possessive NP is a subject.
e. Low accessibility nontransient anchoreds.
f. Pure possession (no restrictions on information status and forms coding the entities)

Once we abandon the idea of characterizing the discourse profiles of possessive NPs, and replace the detailed, lower order generalizations about their distribution with a more abstract definition of their discourse function, we can reach a characterization that is true in 100% of the cases. Note that some features of the prototype we simply characterize differently (e.g., for anchored entities, instead of "new" I am suggesting "low accessibility"; for pronominal anchors, instead of "paragraph-anaphoric", I am suggesting "high accessibility"). But some features simply have to be removed from the characterization, so the discourse function is less specific than the discourse profile (e.g., the humanness of the anchors, the nonprominence of the anchored entities, nonsubject status). In fact, the findings previously presented indicate that in terms of their discourse functions, there is nothing special about both NPs in possessive NPs. Both the anchor and the anchored obey the form-function correlations established by Accessibility Theory, whereby relatively short and uninformative forms (pronouns in this case) code a relatively high degree of accessibility and full or informative definite forms (lexical NPs in this case) code a relatively low degree of accessibility. This means that despite their identifiable discourse prototypical profile, possessive NPs do not even require a separate characterization of the information statuses of the NPs involved.[9] Their component NPs (pronouns and lexical NPs) carry the same discourse functions they code when used independently. What is crucial, then, is that there should be a compatibility between the degree of accessibility of the mental entity referred to and the NP form chosen.

ACCESSIBILITY MARKING, DISCOURSE PROFILES, DISCOURSE FUNCTIONS AND PSYCHOLOGICAL REALITY

Elegant or Inelegant Competence?

What is the relevant level of abstraction speakers and addressees actually operate with? The findings in the previous section show that very often, we cannot distinguish empirically between the predictions of the discourse function and discourse

[9]But, of course, the requirement that some asymmetric association obtain between the two entities referred to remains.

profile approaches. Both account for the (prototypical) data equally well. However, as I previously argued, although linguistic change and grammaticizations attest to the working of prototypical discourse profiles, the totality of synchronic language use is actually better accounted for by a higher generalization—the discourse function. Only the former can account for the formulaity involved in the prototypical cases, but only the latter can account for the flexibility and novelty found in natural discourse, responsible for minority cases that cannot be subsumed under the prototypical case. Because the actual discourse distributions of linguistic expressions are more varied than their prototypical discourse profiles would predict, speakers must at least have recourse to more than one prototypical set of conditions per linguistic form (see 8 again).

However, what kind of knowledge we should attribute to the native speaker at any given point in time is not quite decided by such arguments. The traditional tendency in linguistics has been to argue for a single high-level generalization (i.e., the discourse function abstraction), based on the fact that it is only that generalization that can account for the total linguistic behavior of the native speaker (see the analysis in the previous section). This is in line with both the generative grammarian's and Gricean approaches, which aspire only for the highest, most economical and elegant generalizations. However, it is conceivable that the human mind does not actually operate with the absolutely highest generalizations that linguists can abstract away from the data (see e.g., Armstrong et al., 1983). Bates, Thal, Finlay, and Clancy (2003) emphasized the human ability (even prenatally!) to learn statistically significant patterns. A second option could then be that instead of one unified, abstract generalization, a set of lower-level, more concrete and detailed interpretative strategies are memorized and applied by speakers in connection with constructions, which are defined quite concretely rather than abstractly (see Comrie, 1994; Fillmore, Kay, & O'Connor, 1988; Langacker, 1988). For example, Thompson (2001) has forcefully argued that what are taken to be general constructions (e.g., *that* complements) are in fact recurring patterns which are heavily contrained lexically. This could mean that a number of discourse profiles are enumerated per linguistic form (as proprosed by Fox, 1987), as in the previous (8).

Perhaps the most plausible option is also the least "elegant" one. It combines the two alternatives previously mentioned: Speakers store both the abstract discourse function(s) of the form or construction, as well as its variety of instantiations or discourse profiles, or at least the prototypical discourse profiles. Under this view, although speakers do represent the high generalization about linguistic forms, and although it informs some of their uses, they often rely on local, conventionalized strategies when producing and understanding linguistic forms. Thus, Langacker (1988) argued that grammar contains both highly general schemas and redundant, idiosyncratic formulas. A reasonable variant of the universal "double storage" alternative is that whereas the unified, abstract discourse function or meaning is activated for infrequent linguistic forms, frequent forms are produced and processed more readily by reference to their sets of discourse profiles. Or perhaps, only frequent discourse profiles of frequent forms are directly represented or stored as independent constructions by speakers, whereas infrequent discourse profiles (of frequent forms too) result from the application of the high-level generalization directly. This would be in line with Bybee and Thompson's (2000, p. 381) morphological and syntactic point that "high frequency sequences take on a life of their own"(see also Bybee 1998, 2001).

I doubt that linguistic usage alone can decide between these alternatives. Although I believe the arguments put forth in the last section argue against the possibility that the prototypical discourse profiles are the only representation available to speakers (at least for English prenominal possessive NPs), the findings in the previous section do support a discourse profile model within competence, whereby low-level form-function correlations are stored and used by speakers directly. I am therefore proposing we consider the "redundant storage" alternatives just mentioned. I see a clear role for psycholinguistic research here.

Processing Accessibility Markers: Concrete Discourse Profiles or Abstract Discourse Functions

Psycholinguistic experiments on the processing of referring expressions manipulate distinctions akin to those between discourse profiles–namely, concrete, low-level generalizations. The discourse profiles involved are seen as processing cues, and the relevant interpretations as the processing strategies. But the same question we raised about linguistic analyses can be raised re the psycholinguistic analyses of linguistic forms. Is it the discourse profile that is directly guiding the subjects' interpretations in the experiments, or is it the higher-level discourse function?

Typically, an experiment would compare processing times of one type of referring expression in two types of contexts, and determine that one of them is the default case, because reference in that context is processed faster, or the specific interpretation is processed first no matter what, even when another contextual interpretation is actually called for, so the first one has to be actively rejected. Some psycholinguists then see their results as testifying to the validity of a higher generalization (e.g., Gernsbacher & Shroyer, 1989; Sanford & Garrod, 1981), so that the distinct contexts or discourse profiles that they tested for are merely instantiations of the general (discourse function) claim. Others see their findings as directly reflecting the strategies with which speakers actually operate within real time (e.g., Garnham, Oakhill, & Cruttenden, 1992; Garrod, Freudenthal, & Boyle, 1994; MacDonald & MacWhinney, 1990; Maes, 1996; Maes & Noordman, 1995; McDonald & MacWhinney, 1995; Rinck & Bower, 1995; inter alia). Such theoretical conclusions parallel the preferences for discourse functions and discourse profiles, respectively, in linguistic analyses.

We therefore face a problem with the psycholinguistic "discourse profile strategies" approach, which is similar to the problem of focusing on prototypical discourse profiles.[10] Which approach is to be preferred? The low-level cues approach seems useful when the case under examination involves only one contextual factor that is relevant or dominant (e.g., focus, parallelism), or else, when all or most contextual factors converge on pointing to the same choice of antecedent or referring expression (e.g., when the anaphor is a pronoun and the antecedent is the topic, which also occurs in a parallel grammatical role). Only in such supposedly prototypical cases can a specific strategy apply in full force or not apply at all. Thus, the strategies proposed by psycholinguists are suitable for simple cases, but in actual discourse, at least some cases are more complex. Many production and interpretative situations are not prototypical in that one (or some) factor(s) should trigger one "automatic" (or preferred) strategy, whereas other contextual factors should trigger a different "automatic" (or preferred) strategy.[11] The different distributions of gaps and resumptive pronouns in relative clauses are a case in point.

In Ariel (1999), I established that the distribution of gaps and resumptive pronouns in Hebrew relative clauses is highly correlated with a few factors or discourse profiles: (a) the grammatical role of the relativized NP (the NP role in the relative clause that is coreferent with the head NP –see Keenan & Comrie, 1977), (b) the distance between the head and the relativized NP position, (c) the complexity of the head NP, (d) the obligatoriness or optionality of the role of the relativized NP, and (e) the restrictive or nonrestrictive distinction between relative clauses. Thus, if the relativized NP is a subject, there is a very high chance that a gap will be preferred over a resumptive pronoun (92% of the cases). The same is true when the head and the relativized position are relatively close to each other (93%), when the relative clause is restrictive (100%), and when the head is noncomplex (90%). Other grammatical roles, distant relativized positions, complex heads and nonrestrictive relative clauses have a much stronger tendency to contain resumptive pronouns, although the ratios there are significantly lower. The percentages for gaps seem high enough to merit the status of automatic strategies, dictating the choice of gaps with subjects, close by heads, and so on (and similarly, the association with the subject, or a close by NP as head when a gap is used).

However, what form should one choose if the case is not "prototypical" but "mixed"; for example, the relativized position is a subject (favoring a gap), but the relative clause is nonrestrictive (favoring a resumptive pronoun), or if the distance is relatively large (a pronoun is preferred), but the relative clause is re-

---

[10] I am here ignoring contradictory results, which certainly undermine the strength of the strategies approach (see Cacciari, Carreiras, & Barbolini Cionini, 1997; Garnham et al., 1992; Greene, Gerrig, McKoon, & Ratcliff, 1994 for contradicting results as to gender cues). Also ignored here is the problem of referential (rather than anaphoric) uses, for example, where no explicit antecedent occurs in the discourse, and the addressee is required to retrieve it from his encyclopedic knowledge, or else construct it on the spot. Note that such referring expressions are undistinguishable in their form from expressions used anaphorically, but the "concrete strategies" approach is useless, in fact misleading in such cases.

[11] Note that unlike the psycholinguists, who focus on the addressee, I take the strategies approach to equally apply to the speaker and the addressee.

strictive (a gap is preferred), and so on? Many such "nonhomogenous" combinations of the factors or potential cues previously mentioned occur in natural language. Only 18 of the 77 cases (23.4%) in my data were absolute, in that all the previous factors pointed to the same preference for either a gap or a resumptive pronoun. The majority of the cases did not produce a homogenous profile of an overall high or an overall low accessibility. They combined factors favoring resumptive pronouns and factors favoring gaps. This is why even though it is true that most subjects of relative clauses were realized by gaps, 8% of the subjects did take resumptive pronouns nonetheless. Similarly, even though most close by heads were realized by gaps, 7% were realized by resumptive pronouns, and although obligatory relativized NPs mostly took gaps, 12% did receive a resumptive pronoun. These were all cases where the other factors worked in the opposite direction, of course.

In other words, natural data involve decisions that cannot always be made based on a strategy that hinges on a single cue or an assumed convergence of many cues. As previously demonstrated, I have repeatedly found that what accounts best for referential choices is a complex overall evaluation of degree of accessibility, rather than single cues (see especially Ariel, 1990, 1999, 2001). And these separate factors or cues do not necessarily cluster together to form a strong prototypical case. Thus, once we compute degree of accessibility, based on a number of factors contributing to either high or low degrees of accessibility (all the factors previously noted are associated with either high or low degrees of accessibility), we can better account for the distribution of gaps and resumptive pronouns in Hebrew.[12] Given that gaps code a very high degree of accessibility, whereas (resumptive) pronouns code a relatively lower degree of accessibility, the accessibility prediction is that when the overall degree of accessibility is very high, gaps will be used, whereas when the overall degree of accessibility is relatively lower, a resumptive pronoun will be chosen. This prediction is borne out by the data (Ariel, 1999). In the terminology of this article, the higher discourse function generalization (degree of accessibility) accounts for the data better than any concrete strategy based on discourse profiles, (the high correlations previously noted).[13]

---

[12] Note, however, that I am not claiming that speakers and addressees actually calculate degree of accessibility by considering each of the factors identified as affecting accessibility. It is quite possible that we can assess accessibility levels by monitoring levels of activation directly, even though the latter result from the workings of the accessibility factors discussed here and elsewhere in this literature.

[13] Note that there is a difference (though no incompatibility) between my description of an interaction between conflicting contextual factors and that of Bates and MacWhinney (1982, 1989). In the cases described by Bates and MacWhinney, one factor is stronger and wins out. In cases where we assess degree of accessibility, factors are weighted together, and the overall degree of accessibility determines the NP form chosen.

Although the grammatical cues considered in the gap versus resumptive pronoun case seem insufficient cues despite their high predictive power, some grammatical distinctions should supply (almost) full-proof interpretative strategies. These constitute perfect low-level cues, which could eliminate the need to check for the general discourse function of the referential form. Still, experiments have shown that even these cues are not always used alone (at least not immediately). If any grammatical coding is translatable into an automatic processing strategy, it would seem that gender is. Ehrlich (1980) and Sanford and Garrod (1981) are among those who espoused a gender strategy, namely, that one should first of all look for an antecedent that bears the same gender as the pronoun. This antecedent is rejected only if world knowledge instructs us that this coreference is implausible. Yet if so, how come Sanford and Garrod (1981) cited the following (invented) example as difficult for comprehenders?:

9. a. The donkey$_i$ kicked its owner$_j$ on the leg.
   b. It$_i$ ran into the village and hid.
   c. He$_j$ was extremely annoyed by this aggressive behavior.

After all, the gender cue for *He* is there, and comprehenders should immediately choose 'the owner', rather than 'the donkey' as the intended antecedent. Garrod and Sanford (1982) also found that a gender marked pronoun (e.g., *she*) took longer to process than a name (e.g., *Mary*) to retrieve a gendered antecedent, when the antecedent was part of a conjoined NP, where the nonantecedent was of a different gender, (e.g., *John and Mary*), and hence, did not constitute a competing antecedent. Sanford and Garrod (1985) found a difference in the speed with which subjects processed a pronoun referring to a main versus a subsidiary character, despite the existence of a gender cue. These differences are surprising if a gender-based strategy exists. In all these cases, a gender strategy alone should have enabled a very quick identification of the appropriate antecedent. Nonetheless, subjects seem reluctant to rely on it alone. Arguably, overall accessibility evaluations slowed subjects down.

Another reason to doubt that only automatic low-level strategies are employed in processing is the different processing times associated with different strategies. Apriori, there is no reason to expect that different strategies will take different processing times, provided they are equally reliable. For example, one can sum up the parallelism strategies discussed by Chambers and Smyth (1998) as:

11. Parallel-function strategies:
   a. When encountering a pronoun in a highly parallel construction, assume that the antecedent is coded by the same grammatical role (subject pronouns pick subject antecedents and direct object pronouns pick direct object antecedents).
   b. When encountering a lexical NP in a highly parallel construction, assume that the antecedent is coded by a different grammatical role (subjects pick direct objects, direct objects pick subjects).

If all there is to anaphora resolution is following such practical strategies, why is it that the accessing of the preferred antecedents under the previous strategies is faster for strategy (a) (1861, 1878 msec's) than for strategy (b) (2063, 2160 msec's)? If addresses are merely performing interpretations according to cues, no processing difference should occur. Why should it take longer to search for a different grammatical role than for the same grammatical role? If any difference is expected, subjects (as opposed to direct objects) should have taken less time across the board. The only way to explain the differences in the speed of the application of strategy (a) versus (b) is by reference to a notion of degree of accessibility. The discourse function of pronouns is a high degree of accessibility, whereas that of lexical NPs is lower accessibility. Pronouns are therefore used when the antecedents are more highly accessible to the addressee. Because pronouns are governed by strategy (a), and lexical NPs by strategy (b), applying strategy (a) takes a shorter amount of time.

Note that if, as I am claiming, there is an interaction between various factors affecting referential choices, we should expect experimental results to reflect this. Unfortunately, psycholinguists have tended not to experiment with such cases. Yet, I believe that the experiments reported in Sanford and Garrod (1981) attested to such an interaction. Sanford and Garrod found that it took subjects the same amount of time to process a distant topic as it took them to process a close by nontopical entity (13 and 14 sec for pronouns and definite descriptions, respectively). If subjects employ one strategy at a time in some order, then one of these cases (either the topic or the close by antecedent) should have taken them less time (i.e., the case where the first strategy gives the right answer). But the convergence in processing time is compatible with the assumption that distance and topicality interact with each other (by affecting degree of accessibility, the discourse function), and do not simply constitute two distinct strategies (based on two discourse profiles), applied in isolation in some order.

Last, the fast working of low-level strategies does not only depend on the convergence of processing factors. It is also only feasible when there is a complete complementary distribution between referential forms. When there is such a complementarity, one can be confident in applying the strategy involved. Although this may be (almost) true if one takes as complementary a complex (discourse function) notion of degree of accessibility, if one adopts a one cue or one discourse profile approach, many anaphoric expressions in fact occur in contrastive distribution, potentially retrieving the same entities. Because definite descriptions and pronouns tend to retrieve different antecedents (according to Accessibility Theory the latter retrieve antecedents of a higher degree of accessibility), the strategies associated with them must distinguish between them. However, the difference between them is neutralized in some contexts (as in the Sanford & Garrod, 1981 experiment previously reported on). Similarly, Gernsbacher and Shroyer (1989) found a definitely significant difference between *this* NP antecedents and *a* NP antecedents. Although more zeroes and pronouns referred to *this* NP antecedents than to *a* NP antecedents, and more full NP anaphors referred to *a* NP antecedents than to *this* NP antecedents, still, pronouns, zeros, and full NPs all referred to both types of antecedents (albeit at different ratios). Now, one could counter that such findings simply do not merit an interpretative or production strategy. That may well be true, but one needs to make sure that all single cue strategies are indeed based on cases where a single cue makes two forms be in a complementary distribution. In fact, based on experiments that tested for topicality, gender and verb bias cues, Garrod et al. (1994, pp. 54–5) concluded that there is no one crucial cue.

To find out whether people rely on concrete and detailed discourse profiles (strategies) or on the more abstract discourse function when interpreting referring expressions, experiments must be designed to specifically address this question. It is no easy matter to distinguish experimentally between the cues approach and the discourse function approach. If the cues sought are those allowing for a very fast retrieval, then one may not be able to differentiate between the working of an automatic (discourse profile) cue and simply a very high degree of accessibility (the discourse function), because both are predicted to enable a very fast retrieval. For example, the fact that topics, parallel grammatical roles, and close by antecedents are accessed fast by pronouns could result from the fact that there are specific strategies that are responsible for these retrievals. Alternatively this could be due to the fact that these contexts afford a very high degree of accessibility to the antecedents, and pronouns direct addressees to such contexts (high accessibility is their discourse function). Online experiments should therefore involve contexts that can tease apart the two options.

One such context is where a high degree of accessibility does not result from a common pattern, namely, a case where no cue is plausible. A high degree of accessibility predicts a fast retrieval, but the lack of a consistent discourse profile entails that there is no automatic interpretative strategy available, and retrieval should then be relatively slow. For example, linguists have noted that references to entities previously coded as subjects are very common, especially by pronouns and especially when the anaphoric expression is itself a subject (Du Bois, 1987; Halmari, 1996). Not so for direct objects. But what if the direct object is for some other reason very accessible (e.g., it is the discourse topic)? Most probably, it would be the preferred antecedent (for a pronoun). Now, if processing time in this case should be slower, similar to that required when accessing antecedents not according to set strategies, this would support the discourse profile strategy assumption. Perhaps interpreters first considered the grammatical subject as the intended antecedent, rejected it as contextually inappropriate, and only then opted for the direct object. If, however, highly accessible direct object antecedents are accessed as fast as subjects, then the discourse function pertaining to degree of accessibility is probably the determining factor. Last, if processing highly accessible direct objects is slower than that of processing highly accessible subjects but faster than inaccessible direct objects, this will support a multistrategy assumption. This intermediate result may be interpreted as indicating the simultaneous workings of both mechanisms.

Another context where the different hypotheses can be distinguished is where degree of accessibility is low but the context is recurrent, such that an interpretative discourse profile strategy could be extracted. The discourse profile strategies approach should predict a relatively short processing time (due to the automaticity of the procedure involved), but Accessibility Theory predicts a relatively longer processing time (due to the low degree of accessibility). Initial discourse references to Given entities (new to the discourse, but known by the addressee) could be a case in point. Discourse initially, we commonly have to access antecedents from long-term memory, which takes relatively long, but this is a process we repeatedly perform discourse initially. One can then compare the processing of first-mention Given entities in initial discourse position versus noninitial position. The strategies approach predicts a shorter processing time for the first case. Accessibility Theory predicts a similarity in processing times (though no identity, because of competition with other antecedents in noninitial position).

Another set of relevant experiments might involve the discourse profiles of possessive NPs, mentioned previously. One could compare the processing time of paragraph-internal antecedents with that of global topic antecedents for the anchor. Because the former constitute the prototypical case (close to 90%), they are potentially interpretable by reference to an automatic discourse profile strategy, and should take less time according to such an approach. According to Accessibility Theory, however, repeatedly mentioned global topics, even if distant, are as highly (if not more) accessible as close-by (transient) nontopics, even though they are not as numerous. There should not be significant processing time differences between the accessing of these two types of antecedents, therefore. Similarly, one can compare between human (frequent) and inanimate (infrequent) anchors, and between inanimate (frequent) and human (infrequent) anchoreds, and so on. The discourse function approach predicts that if the forms examined are properly chosen (by considering their accessibility-based discourse function), there should not be a significant difference in the processing times for different discourse profiles for equally accessible antecedents. The discourse profile approach predicts that some contexts, those interpretable by an automatic discourse profile strategy, should be processed faster than those where the strategy is inapplicable. The third, "inelegant" possibility is that both mechanisms are at work, so that there could theoretically be a four-way distinction between: high accessibility + automatic cue; high accessibility – automatic cue; low accessibility + automatic cue; low accessibility – automatic cue.

In conclusion, I have argued that a (prototypical) discourse profile approach to the usage of linguistic forms (e.g., accessibility markers) is insufficient in and of itself. A discourse function approach better accounts for all the uses of, for example, possessive NPs found in natural discourse (see Ariel, in press for definite descriptions). However, the fact that a single, abstract discourse function can account for all the data, whereas the (prototypical) discourse profiles (alone) cannot, does not rule out the possibility that the actual production and processing of linguistic expressions relies only or at least also on sets of discourse profiles (processing or production strategies), some of which are prototypical. After all, a common linguistic change is for the prototypical discourse profile to become the (new and obligatory) discourse function. I therefore end with a plea for psycholinguists to devise experiments testing the options here addressed: Discourse functions, discourse profiles, or some combination of the two as guiding speakers' and addressees' usage of referring expressions, and linguistic expressions in general.

REFERENCES

Ariel, M. (1985). *Givenness marking*. Unpublished doctoral dissertation, Tel-Aviv University, Tel Aviv, Israel.

Ariel, M. (1988a). Female and male stereotypes in Israeli literature and media: Evidence from introductory patterns. *Language and Communication, 8*, 43–68.

Ariel, M. (1988b). Referring and accessibility. *Journal of Linguistics, 24*, 65–87.

Ariel, M. (1990). *Accessing noun phrase antecedents*. London: Routledge.

Ariel, M. (1996). Referring expressions and the +/- coreference distinction. In T. Fretheim & J.K. Gundel (Eds.), *Reference and referent accessibility* (pp. 13–35). Amsterdam: Benjamins.

Ariel, M. (1999). Cognitive universals and linguistic conventions: The case of resumptive pronouns. *Studies in Language, 23*, 217–269.

Ariel, M. (2001). Accessibility Theory: An overview. In T. Sanders, J. Schilperoord, & W. Spooren (Eds.), *Text representation: Linguistic and psycholinguistic aspects* (pp. 29–87). Amsterdam: Benjamins.

Ariel, M. (2002). Possessive NPs, discourse functions and discourse profiles. In *Proceedings of the 28th annual meeting of the Berkeley Linguistics Society* (pp. 15–26).

Ariel, M. (in press). A grammar in every register?: The case of definite descriptions. In J. Hedberg & R. Zacharsley (Eds.), *Topics on the grammar pragmatics interface: Papers in honor of Jeanette K. Gundel*. Amsterdam: Benjamins.

Ariel, M., & Giora, R. (1998). A self versus other point of view in language: Redefining femininity and masculinity. *International Journal of the Sociology of Language, 129*, 59–86.

Armstrong, S. L., Gleitman, L., & Gleitman, H. (1983). On what some concepts might not be. *Cognition, 13*, 263–309.

Bates, E., & MacWhinney, B. (1989). Functionalism and the competition model. In B. MacWhinney & E. Bates (Eds.), *The crosslinguistic study of sentence processing* (pp. 3–73). Cambridge, England: Cambridge University Press.

Bates, E., Thal, D., Finlay, B. L., & Clancy, B. (2003). Early language development and its neural correlates. In F. Boller & J. Grafman (Series Eds.) & S. J. Segalowitz & I. Rapin (Vol. Eds.), *Handbook of neuropsychology, Vol. 8. Part II, Child neuropsychology* (2nd ed., pp. 525–592). Amsterdam: Elsevier.

Blake, B. (1994). *Case*. Cambridge, England: Cambridge University Press.

Brown, C. (1983). Topic continuity in written English narrative. In Givón (Ed.), *Topic continuity in discourse* (pp. 313–341). Amsterdam: Benjamins.
Bybee, J. (1998). In *Papers from the 34th regional meeting of the Chicago Linguistic Society* (pp. 421–435).
Bybee, J. (2001). Frequency effects on French Liaison. In J. Bybee & P. Hopper (Eds.), *Frequency and the emergence of linguistic structure* (pp. 337–359). Amsterdam: Benjamins.
Bybee, J., & Thompson, S. A. (2000). Three frequency effects in syntax. In *Proceedings of the Twenty-Third Annual Meeting of the Berkeley Linguistic Society* (pp. 378–388).
Cacciari, C., Carreiras, M., & Barbolini Cionini, C. (1997). When words have two genders: Anaphor resolution for Italian functionally ambiguous words. *Journal of Memory and Language, 37*, 517–32.
Chafe, W. L. (1976). Givenness, contrastiveness, definiteness, subjects, topics, and point of view. In C. N. Li (Ed.), *Subject and topic* (pp. 25–57). New York: Academic Press.
Chambers, C. G., & Smyth, R. (1998). Structural parallelism and discourse coherence: A test of centering theory. *Journal of Memory and Language, 39*, 593–608.
Chappell, H. (1996). Inalienability and the personal domain in Mandarin Chinese discourse. In H. Chappell & W. McGregor (Eds.), *The grammar of inalienability* (pp. 465–527). Berlin: Mouton de Gruyter.
Chappell, H., & Thompson, S. A. (1992). The semantics and pragmatics of associative *de* in Mandarin discourse. *C.L.A.O, XXI*, 199–229.
Comrie, B. (1994). Coreference: Between grammar and discourse. In *Proceedings of the eighteenth annual meeting of the Kansai Linguistic Society* (pp. 1–10). Osaka: Kansai Linguistic Society.
Dahl, Ö., & Fraurud, K. (1996). Animacy in grammar and discourse. In Fretheim & Gundel (Eds.), *Reference and referent accessibility* (pp. 47–64). Amsterdam: Benjamins.
Deane, P. (1987). English possessives, topicality, and the Silverstein hierarchy. *BLS, 13*, 65–76.
Deane, P. (1992). *Grammar in the mind and brain: Explorations in cognitive syntax*. Berlin: Mouton de Gruyter.
Du Bois, J. W. (1987). The discourse basis of ergativity. *Language, 63*, 805–855.
Du Bois, J. W. (1988, May). Discourse as pattern model for grammar: The possessor=ergator affiliation. Talk given at the University of Oregon, Eugene, Oregon.
Du Bois, J. W. (2000). Santa Barbara Corpus of Spoken American English, Part one. Three CD-ROMs, distributed by the Linguistic Data Consortium, University of Pennsylvania.
Duranti, A., & Ochs, E. (1990). Genitive constructions and agency in Samoan discourse. *Studies in Language 14*, 1–23.
Ehrlich, K. (1980). Comprehension of pronouns. *Quarterly Journal of Experimental Psychology 32*, 247–255.
Fillmore, C., Kay, P., & O'Connor, C. (1988). Regularity and idiomaticity in grammatical constructions: The case of *let alone*. *Language, 64*, 501–538.
Fox, B. A. (1987). *Discourse structure and anaphora: Written and conversational English.* Cambridge, England: Cambridge University Press.
Fraurud, K. (1996). Cognitive ontology and NP form. In Fretheim & Gundel (Eds.), *Reference and referent accessibility* (pp. 65–87). Amsterdam: Benjamins.
Fretheim, T., & Gundel, J. K. (Eds.). (1996). *Reference and referent accessibility*. Amsterdam: Benjamins.
Garnham, A., Oakhill, J., & Cruttenden, H. (1992). The role of implicit causality and gender cue in the interpretation of pronouns. *Language and Cognitive Processes, 7*, 231–255.
Garrod, S., Freudenthal, D., & Boyle, E. (1994). The role of different types of anaphor in the on-line resolution of sentences in a discourse. *Journal of Memory and Language 33*, 39–68.
Garrod, S., & Sanford, A. J. (1982). The mental representation of discourse in a focused memory system: Implications for the interpretation of anaphoric noun phrases. *Journal of Semantics 1*, 21–41.
Gernsbacher, M. A., & Shroyer, S. (1989). The cataphoric use of indefinite this in spoken narratives. *Memory and Cognition 17*, 536–40.

Gibbs, R. W. (1990). Comprehending figurative referential descriptions. *Journal of Experimental Psychology: Learning, Memory and Cognition, 16*, 56–66.

Givón, T. (1983a). Topic continuity in spoken English. In Givón (Ed.), *Topic continuity in discourse* (pp. 343–363). Amsterdam: Benjamins.

Givón, T. (Ed.). (1983b). *Topic continuity in discourse*. Amsterdam: Benjamins.

Greene, S. B., Gerrig, R. J., McKoon, G., & Ratcliff, R. (1994). Unheralded pronouns and management by common ground. *Journal of Memory and Language 33*, 511–526.

Halmari, H. (1996). On accessibility and coreference. In Fretheim & Gundel (Eds.), *Reference and referent accessibility* (pp. 155–178). Amsterdam: Benjamins.

Hawkins, R. (1981). Towards an account of the possessive construction: NP's N and the N of NP. *Journal of Linguistics, 17*, 247–269.

Heine, B. (1997). *Possession: Cognitive sources, forces, and grammaticalization*. Cambridge, England: Cambridge University Press.

Hobbs, J. R. (1976). Pronoun resolution. Research report 76–7, Dept. of Computer Sciences, City College, City University of New York.

Jucker, A.H. (1996). News actor labelling in British newspapers. *Text, 16* (3), 373–390.

Karmiloff-Smith, A. (1985). Language and cognitive processes from a developmental perspective. *Language and Cognitive Processes ,1*, 61–85.

Keenan, E. L., & Comrie, B. (1977). Noun phrase accessibility and universal grammar. *Linguistic Inquiry, 8*, 63–99.

Langacker, R. W. (1988). A usage-based model. In B. Rudzka-Ostyn (Ed.), *Topics in Cognitive Linguistics* (pp. 127–161). Amsterdam: Benjamins.

Langacker, R. W. (1991). *Foundations of cognitive grammar, Vol. 2*. Stanford, CT: Stanford University Press.

Lehmann, C. (1985). Ergative and active traits in Latin. In F. Plank (Ed.), *Relational typology* (pp. 243–255). Berlin: Mouton Publishers.

Lord, C., & Dahlgren, K. (1997). Participant and event anaphora in newspaper articles. In J. Bybee, J. Haiman, & S. A. Thompson (Eds.), *Essays on language function and language type dedicated to T. Givón* (pp. 323–356). Amsterdam: Benjamins.

MacDonald, M., & MacWhinney, B. (1990). Measuring inhibition and facilitation from pronouns. *Journal of Memory and Language, 29*, 469–492.

Maes, A. A. (1996). The markedness of abstract-object anaphors in discourse. In W. de Mulder & L. Tasmowski (Eds.), *Coherence and anaphora. Belgian Journal of Linguistics, 10*, 161–183.

Maes, A. A., & Noordman, L. G. M. (1995). Demonstrative nominal anaphors: A case of non-identificational markedness. *Linguistics ,33*, 255–282.

Mann, W. C., & Thompson, S. A. (Eds.). (1992). *Discourse description: Diverse linguistic analyses of a fund-raising text*. Amsterdam: Benjamins.

McDonald J. L., & MacWhinney, B. (1995). The time course of anaphor resolution: Effects of implicit verb causality and gender. *Journal of Memory and Language 34*, 543–566.

Morris, C. (1994). *Bearing witness*. Boston: Little, Brown.

Norman, D., Rumelhart, D. E., & the LNR Research Group (Eds.). (1975). *Explorations in cognition*. San Francisco: Freeman.

Onishi, K. H., & Murphy, G. L. (1993). Metaphoric reference: When metaphors are not understood as easily as literal expressions. *Memory and Cognition, 21*, 763–772.

Osselton, N. E. (1988). Thematic genitives. In G. Nixon & J. Honey (Eds.), *An historic tongue* (pp. 138–144). London: Routledge.

Prince, E. F. (1992). The ZPG letter: Subjects, definiteness, and information-status. In W.C. Mann & S.A. Thompson (Eds.), *Discourse description: Diverse linguistic analyses of a fund-raising text* (pp. 295–325). Amsterdam: Benjamins.

Quirk, R., Leech, G. N., & Svartvik, J. (1972). *A grammar of contemporary English*. London: Longman.

Rinck, M., & Bower, G. H. (1995). Anaphora resolution and the focus of attention in situation models. *Journal of Memory and Language, 34*, 110–131.

Rumelhart, D. E., & Levin, J. A. (1975). A language comprehension system. In N. Rumelhart & the LNR research group (Eds.), 179–208.

Sanford, A. J., & Garrod, S. C. (1981). *Understanding written language*. Chichester, England: Wiley.

Sanford, A. J., & Garrod, S.C. (1985). On the real-time character of interpretation during reading. *Language and Cognitive Processes, 1*, 43-49.

Taylor, J. R. (1994). "Subjective" and "objective" readings of possessor nominals. *Cognitive Linguistics, 5*, 201–242.

Taylor, J. R. (1996). *Possessives in English*. Oxford, England: Clarendon.

Thompson, S. (2001). Constructions and conversation. Paper presented at the 10th Conference on Concepetual Structure, Discourse and Language, Univeristy of Santa Barbara, CA.

Toole, J. (1996). The effect of genre on referential choice. In T. Fretheim and J. K. Gundel (Eds.), *Reference and referent accessibility* (pp. 263–290). Amsterdam: Benjamins.

DISCOURSE PROCESSES, *37*(2), 117–144

Reference Management in Instructive Discourse

Alfons Maes
Communication and Cognition Group
Tilburg University, The Netherlands

Anja Arts
Discourse Studies Group
Tilburg University, The Netherlands

Leo Noordman
Discourse Studies Group
Tilburg University, The Netherlands

This article investigates the effect of 2 language-in-use factors on the introduction and maintenance of referents in instructive discourse. These factors, implemented as conditions in an instructive production task, were the assumed visual identity for the reader of the objects or referents to be referred to in the instructions (*visually same* vs. *visually different*) and the assumed goal of the reader (*reading to do* vs. *reading to learn*).

The results show that both factors have a strong impact on the writers' referential behavior. *Visually same* referents are introduced and reintroduced fairly systematically by means of perceptually overspecified NPs. *Visually different* referents are introduced systematically by extra propositional identification speech acts and they are reintroduced more often by attenuated anaphoric expressions. Apart from that, writers show a number of referential strategies which fit in with the assumed reader's goal. Writers in the *reading to learn* condition use more overspecified expressions than writers in the *reading to do* condition.

The results contribute to a more comprehensive understanding of the factors that determine the form of referential expressions in discourse. Referential expressions which are more informative than necessary for identification purposes do not only occur when the activation level of discourse referents is low, but also when the writer anticipates specific conditions in which the information will be used by the reader.

Correspondence and requests for reprints should be sent to Alfons Maes, Communication and Cognition Group, Faculty of Arts, Tilburg University, P.O. Box 90153, 5000 LE Tilburg NL. E-mail:

The main goal of recent theories of discourse reference, such as Accessibility (e.g., Ariel, 1990), Centering (e.g., Grosz, Joshi, & Weinstein, 1995) or Givenness (e.g., Gundel, Hedberg, & Zacharski, 1993), is to provide an explanatory account of the relation between types of referential expressions on the one hand, and degrees of mental activation of discourse referents on the other. The general idea is that referential expressions need more coding material as the referent is less activated and vice versa. In analytical as well as experimental reference research, a large number of factors are uncovered, which are considered to affect the activation level of discourse referents. These factors can be distinguished into different levels: on the one hand surface level characteristics of discourse, such as order of mention (Gernsbacher & Hargreaves, 1988), sentence position, syntactic role (e.g., Gordon, Grosz, & Gilliom, 1993; Gordon, Hendrick, Ledoux, & Yang, 1999), depth of embedding (Gordon & Hendrick, 1997; Ward, Sproat, & McKoon, 1991), competing candidates or referential distance (Ariel, 1988); on the other hand more conceptual characteristics, such as the conceptual structure of discourse in terms of episode shifts (Anderson, Garrod, & Sanford, 1983), protagonist-hood (Francik, 1985), thematic structure (Vonk, Hustinx, & Simons, 1992) or topicality (Morrow, 1985). Apart from that, intricate combinations of surface and conceptual factors are studied, such as morphological gender and conceptual content (Carreiras & Gernsbacher, 1992) or morphological gender and pragmatic-conceptual inferences (Garrod, Freudenthal, & Boyle, 1994).

Research into the mental activation of discourse referents attempts to disentangle the way in which language users distribute and manage their mental attention over referents, a process which is highly determined by the limitations of working memory. A number of heuristics which we use in interpreting referential expressions suggest that attention management is guided by referential economy and efficiency. One such heuristic is the propensity not to expect or use more referential material than necessary to uniquely identify a discourse referent. Another heuristic is that we expect discourse referents to be introduced in their full form and afterwards reintroduced in weakened forms, which is why (1) and not (2) sounds natural to us:

(1) John is back home again. He traveled through Asia for the last 5 months.
(2) ?He/John is back home again. John traveled through Asia for the last 5 months.

These intuitions make clear that using referential expressions to efficiently activate referents is a solid part of our discourse competence. Yet, they also suggest that referential expressions are monofunctional, which is not. Referential expressions can display additional functions. One such function is adding new information about referents, as is shown in empirical (e.g., Almor, 1999) as well as analytical studies (e.g., Maes & Noordman, 1995). Likewise, one can easily collect referential phenomena which deviate from the idea of economic activation. If for example a novelist decides to introduce and maintain his character by using a pronoun only, if children never talk about their mother by using a pronoun or if defendants and plaintiffs in Flemish court orders are hardly ever pronominalized (Maes, 1991), apparently other than economic activation considerations come into play.

One can take up different theoretical positions to deal with these "non-standard uses" of referential expressions. On the one hand, one can claim that they are all (deliberate) violations of the basic activation pattern. On the other hand, one can think of different basic systems which—in interaction—are responsible for the use of referential expressions. Apart from activation, one can think of a number of performance based aspects of discourse, such as discourse goals, types of relationships between discourse participants, different modes of communication and situational conditions. These aspects can be seen as parameters with different settings, the interaction of which explains referential patterns and strategies in any specific language-in-use context. So, applied to the previous example, a pronoun introducing a main character in a novel can be looked at as being peculiar and deviant, because it violates normal activation procedures of referential expressions, or as normal, given our prior knowledge about specific narrative (literary) conventions and strategies used by novelists.

It is difficult to determine at this moment which theoretical position is the most sensible one. We first need more systematized, controlled, and generalizable knowledge about the language-in-use factors that affect reference, about the interaction of these factors and their effect on referential patterns and strategies.

This article intends to contribute to this type of knowledge. It focuses on a discourse type which is preeminently affected by performance factors, that is, instructions for use. Instructions for use typically intermediate between the mental representation of users on the one hand and the physical execution of tasks on the other. They support the execution of tasks, such as the installation and tuning of computer, video and camera equipment or household appliances, and they imply that users manipulate objects in a physical task environment. In designing these instructions, writers have to take into account the relevant characteristics of users and tasks, and have to assume specific goals, levels of experience, prior knowledge and task conditions of the readers or users. Practice and research in the field of instructive text design uncovers a large number of textual variables which are related to these conditions of use (see e.g., Jansen & Maes, 1999).

In this article, we discuss the results of a production experiment, set up to elicit referential strategies in instructions for use. The experimental conditions were varied along the lines of two language-in-use variables: the goal of the reader (*reading to do* versus *reading to learn*) and the visual identity of the referents to be referred to in the instruction task (*visually same* versus *visually different* referents).

In the next section, we discuss the relevance of instructive discourse for reference research and in particular the relevance of the performance factors used. After that, we discuss the set up and results of the production experiment.

REFERENTIAL EXPRESSIONS IN INSTRUCTIONS

Reference Research and Instructions

Instructions for use mediate between users, their goals and representations on the one hand, and the task context on the other. This results in referential expressions performing multiple functions. They not only have to enable users to establish, maintain, conceptualize and mentally locate discourse referents within the ongoing mental representation of text and task, but they also have to spatially locate them within the relevant perceptual environment of the task. This characteristic poses a complex and specific referential task for readers and writers.

From the viewpoint of the reader, the location of referents is a necessary prerequisite for any successful execution of tasks. According to recent research by Glenberg and Robertson (1999), actively locating referents (in their terms: indexing words to objects) facilitates task performance and comprehension considerably, as it enables readers to derive affordances from these indexed objects, which in turn are to be meshed into a coherent (i.e., doable and envisionable) set of actions (1999, p. 7). These affordances, which arise from the interaction of an observer and an object, "are ways in which an observer can interact with an object, and they are presumed to arise, to a great degree, from perceptual processes" (1999, p. 4). On the basis of the results of a performance experiment, they claim that this perceptually based background knowledge represents an important complement of abstract semantic knowledge in constructing mental representations.

From the viewpoint of the writer, the location of referents requires the construction of an appropriate description on the basis of available descriptive ingredients. Objects can be located by using perceptual (e.g., color, size, shape) or locative (e.g., dimensional axis, direction) characteristics of objects, and by using expressions which imply (or not) the comparison between different objects (e.g., *the larger button* versus *the red button*). Apart from that, writers can take many different other perspectives in identifying referents: the user function of an object (*the alarm button*), the system function of an object (*the exhaust valve*), the consequence of the actions in the task (*the button that makes the display light up*), the instructor's task (*the round button I mentioned before*), the user's task (*the button you just pushed twice, the button you have to look for*). Together with the normal text based (e.g., anaphors like *this, this button*, or *it*), semantic (*the button*) or knowledge based referential options (*the button that usually carries the label 'time'*), this results in a fairly luxuriant collection of referential strategies in instructive discourse.

The literature shows a number of interesting production studies on reference and perspective taking in task-oriented discourse. Most of these studies focus on spoken dialogue. They rely on collecting data with concurrent feedback facility, visual contact between speaker and listener (e.g., Klein, 1982; Schober, 1995,

1993; Wright, 1990; Yule & Powers, 1994), with indirect, non-visual feedback facility (Beun & Cremers, 1998; Clark & Wilkes-Gibbs, 1986; von Stutterheim & Kohlmann, 1998), or with different variations in language mode and interactivity (e.g., Chapanis, Parrish, Ochsman, & Weeks, 1977; Cohen, 1984; Krauss & Weinheimer, 1966). These studies contain many indications of an instructor adapting referential behavior to the situation in which the dialogue takes place.

An important point of discussion in these studies as well as in this study is the level of specification used to identify referents in different communicative modes (i.e., different degrees of feedback facilities in spoken and written discourse). In general, feedback facility is claimed to result in instructors minimizing their referential efforts by using underdetermined expressions and strategies, that are not necessarily referentially robust, as they rely on the fact that a participating listener is also responsible for successful reference and will ask for clarification if referential problems arise (i.e., the *principle of mutual responsibility* in Clark & Wilkes-Gibbs, 1986). Applied to a nonfeedback situation, this could result in writers overspecifying their references due to their awareness of their "distant" responsibility (Clark & Wilkes-Gibbs, 1986, p. 35). At first sight, this idea seems to be supported by Pechmann's (1989) investigation of instructive production in a nonfeedback spoken context. His results show the opposite of minimization, that is, a large extent of referential overspecification. In his experiment, participants had to identify objects by reacting to visual stimuli. The experimental task made participants identify the referents incrementally, bit by bit, which often resulted in the use of nonparsimonious, overspecified expressions. Consequently, Pechmann explains the overspecification not in terms of the absence of a feedback facility, but in terms of incremental speech production strategies used by adult speakers, thus suggesting a close connection between overspecification and the incremental nature of the spoken medium. Therefore, the explanation in terms of the experimental task is not applicable to the situation of well-considered written production.

Other results seem to support the idea that the spoken medium rather than the feedback facility is the crucial factor in producing overspecified expressions. According to Cohen (1984), instructors produce far more identification information (in particular identification requests) in the spoken (telephone) mode compared to the written (keyboard) mode, although both modes allowed for direct, online feedback.

In sum, we expect that instructive writers in a nonfeedback situation will use a large number of overspecifications, not (only) because of the incremental nature of language production or particular characteristics of the spoken communication mode, but because of the more general principle of distant responsibility.

Within the broader context of discourse reference, this study methodologically contrasts with the large number of studies based on the results of comprehension data. The interpretation of the production data used in this study starts from the assumption that a writer anticipates the reader's needs. This means that the data are taken to reflect assumptions on the part of the writer on the cognitive effort needed by the reader to select a referent, a view which is congruent with other production studies on discourse reference (see Fletcher, 1984; Maes, 1997; Marlsen-Wilson, Levy & Tyler, 1982). Furthermore, the nature of the production data contrasts with analytical studies based on real-life texts. Our study opts for elicited data that guarantee much better the control over the performance factors we are interested in.

Visual Identity and Reader's Goal

The experiment focuses on two performance factors that were implemented as independent variables in the experimental writing task. The first was *the assumed visual identity of the objects* to be identified by the reader or user. Participants were asked to assume that the objects to be referred to were either visually the same to their reader (*visually same* condition, henceforth VS), or visually different to the reader (*visually different* condition, henceforth VD). Within the context of learning from (instructive) discourse, the use of visual information is known to be highly relevant. Apart from the results in Glenberg & Robertson (1999), mentioned previously, there is evidence coming from studies in the framework of dual coding theory, which makes it clear (although not always unequivocally) that visual support in comprehending actions pays off in that it helps to build solid mental representations based on the integration of verbal and visual input (e.g., Mayer, Bove, Bryman, Mars, & Tapango, 1996). Likewise, a visual representation can be used to code multiple information units at once and thus reduce working memory load caused by complicated verbal instructions (e.g., Marcus, Cooper, & Sweller, 1996). Apart from this research evidence, the relevance of visuals is shown in technical writing practice: manuals abundantly opt for visuals, which are verbally referred to in many different ways (see for an analysis Maes & Lenting, 1999).

We expect that the visual identity of the task-related objects, together with the general tendency of instructive writers to overspecify in a nonfeedback situation, will have a pervasive influence on the nature of referential strategies. First, writers in the VS condition are expected to use predominantly perception based expressions and perception based overspecifications, whereas writers in the VD condition are expected to use a combination of perception, knowledge and text based strategies. Second, the VS condition is assumed to promote overspecified anaphoric expressions and in particular the use of so-called independent or exophoric anaphoric NPs, that is, anaphors which enable users direct access via the perceptual context, without mediation of the previous linguistic context. A third assumption is based on the observation that writers in the VD condition have a referentially more difficult task. They cannot rely on the presence of the objects in the task scene, and have to expend more referential effort to put an object on the counter before it can be referred to in the actual instructions. One way of tackling the complexity of this task is to use extra identification speech acts, which prepare the object references in the actual instructions. This strategy of using independent identification speech acts is observed under different instructive conditions in Cohen (1984). His participants had to instruct a listener or reader on how to install a water pump, in different communication modes. A striking conclusion in comparing the telephone (spoken) with the keyboard (written) mode, was that instructors in the telephone mode produced a large number of what he called *identification requests*, that is, extra propositional speech acts preceding the actual instructions (e.g., *there is a black o-ring?*). Because direct feedback is possible in both modes and the water pump is identical, Cohen has to conclude that the extra referential effort is connected with the difference between spoken and written language. In view of our experimental set-up, however, one can expect this type of referential behavior to be exhibited mainly by VD writers, in an attempt to solve their referentially more complex task.

The second variable in the experimental task was the *assumed goal of the reader.* Half of the instructive writers had to focus on a reader with a typical *reading to do* goal, that is, the incidental execution of a task (DO condition). The other half had to assume that, by executing the task, the reader intended to learn the task once and for all, that is, a *reading to learn* goal (LEARN condition). Both readers' goals reflect naturalistic and ecologically valid ways of using instructive texts. For example, standard installation and maintenance sections in instructions for use typically represent information which is to be executed incidentally. This information typically fits in with the *reading to do* situation. Conversely, most of the instructions in a computer manual are typically meant to be learned for future application and hence fit in with the *reading to learn* situation. The dichotomy between *reading to do* and *reading to learn* can also be related to different stages in the process of learning skills: In terms of Anderson's ACT*-theory (1983) learning can be associated more with the first, declarative phase of learning, and doing with the other two phases, that is, the associative and autonomous phase. Likewise, learners are known to benefit more than doers from goal-like declarative information in instructive discourse on top of procedural information (see e.g., Kieras & Bovair, 1984, Smith & Goodman, 1984, Ummelen, 1997). Writers appear to shape their instructions in the same vein: writers who focus on a *reading to learn* goal produce more declarative goal information and make declarative information more prominent in the linear organization of their instructions than writers who focus on a *reading to do* goal (Maes, 2000).

The awareness of these two readers' goals is expected to be reflected in the referential behavior of instructive writers as well. *Reading to learn* writers can be expected to produce more coding material (extra propositions or NP-attributes) in referring to objects than *reading to do* writers, because of the differences in assessment of the importance of the referential task with regard to the reader. Likewise, writers focused on immediate, one-shot task execution are expected to use more direct, that is, perception based conceptualization strategies, whereas writers with learning users in mind most likely use relatively more knowledge based strategies aimed at providing meaningful (i.e., functional, task-oriented, system-oriented) insight in task and device.

In sum, the two independent variables are expected to have the following effects on the referential behavior of instructive writers:

Visual identity. (a) Participants in the VS condition use more perception based expressions and more overspecified perception based expressions than participants in the VD condition, (b) Participants in the VS condition use more overspecified anaphoric expressions than participants in the VD condition and in particular more "exophoric" anaphoric NPs. (c) Participants in the VD condition use more extra identification propositions (i.e., propositional overspecification) than participants in the VS condition.

Reader's goal. 'Learners' need more and other (types of) information than 'doers'. In particular, we expect the following differences: (a) *Reading to learn* writers use more perceptually overspecified expressions and overspecified anaphoric expressions than *reading to do* writers. (b) *Reading to learn* writers use more nonperception based expressions than *reading to do* writers.

METHOD

Task

The experimental production task consisted in writing a fax to a friend with instructions on how to use a radio alarm. The fax had to be directed either to a *reading to do* or a *reading to learn* reader, and either to a reader with exactly the *same* radio alarm or a *different* specimen. For these situations, we constructed specific scenarios, which were presented to the participants as follows:

Reading-to-do scenario. Your friend is staying just for one night in the room of someone who is not at home. He needs to get up early the next morning. In the room he has found a radio alarm, but not a user's manual. Send him a clear answer by fax to the following question: How do I program, just for this one time, the radio alarm in such a way that I will be in time for my appointment tomorrow morning?

Reading to learn scenario. Your friend received a radio alarm from his sister. He wants to use it in the future to get up every morning, but he did not receive a user's manual. Send him a clear answer by fax to the following question: How do I learn to program, *once and for all*, the radio alarm in such a way that, from now on, I will be in time for my appointments in the morning?

Same radio alarm scenario. The radio alarm that your friend found in the apartment or received from his sister is identical to the one you have.

Different radio alarm scenario. The radio alarm that your friend found in the apartment or received from his sister, is shaped like a toy bear.

Material

Participants received a booklet with the following information. (a) An introductory page on the purpose of this writing task. The task was said to be part of an investigation of the way in which experienced writers describe instructions that are presented in a visual fashion. Participants were asked to use only plain text, consisting of paragraphs and full sentences; and they were asked to be fully explicit, and to write correctly. (b) The scenario description of the experimental task, in one of four versions (reading to do & same radio alarm, reading to learn & same radio alarm, reading to do & different radio alarm, reading to learn & different radio alarm). (c) The visual representation of the radio alarm participants had to focus on (see Figure 1). (d) Instructions for using the radio alarm (for a fragment, see Figure 2). The instructions as a whole described four functions to be performed with the radio alarm (how to set the clock and alarm time, how to activate the alarm, how to turn off the alarm, how to doze off with the radio). Altogether, the instructions contained 42 information slots divided into two information types: *goal information* (26 slots) and *action information* (16 slots). Goal slots were all uniformly presented as a combination of a task verb and an object. Figure 2 contains four goal slots in three hierarchical levels (1 Set time; 2 Set clock time; 3 Set hour/Set minutes). Action slots were presented in visual fashion; each action was represented as a two-row table. Figure 2 contains two action slots. The lower row in each table symbolically represents the buttons on the radio

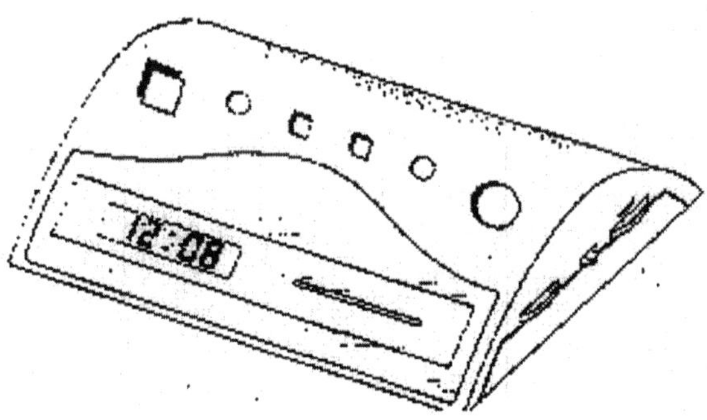

FIGURE 1 Radio alarm

1 SET TIME

1.1 SET CLOCK TIME

1.1.1 SET HOUR

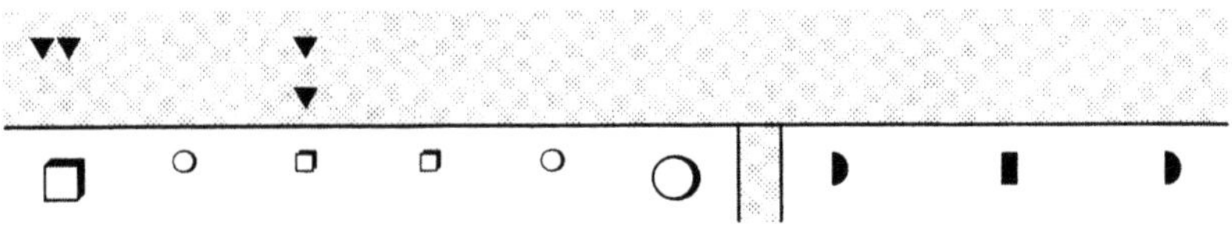

1.1.2 SET MINUTES

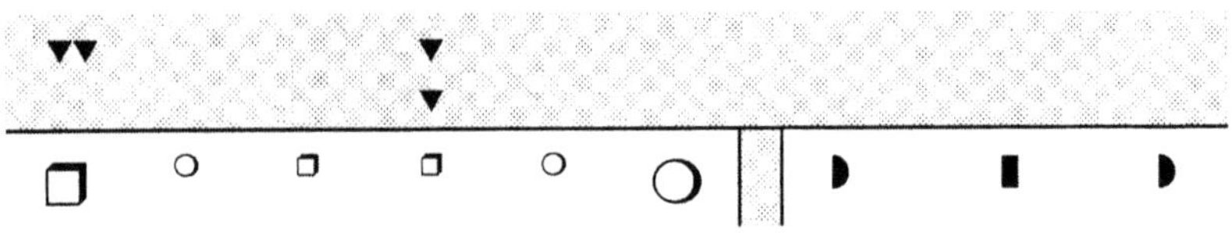

FIGURE 2 Fragment of the instructions in the experimental material. Six information units: four goal slots in three embedded paragraph levels (i.e., the verbal elements or titles), and two action units (i.e., the two visual instructions in table format).

alarm. The upper row contains the instructions. (e) Instructions on how to read the instructions, especially, on how to read the upper row of the action tables. For example, the first action in Figure 2 means that the left button has to be pushed in and held in (i.e., two black triangles horizontally), while pressing the third button repeatedly (i.e., two black triangles vertically). (f) A closing page with a number of personal and task oriented questions.

Participants

In this experiment, 105 participants participated—85 women and 20 men. The participants were all students in their final year of translation college, taking part in a regular advanced Dutch writing course. They were all native speakers of Dutch. Participation in this experiment was part of the course.

Procedure

This experiment was run in sessions of 15 to 20 participants each. Each session took place in a computer room and took about 40 min. The participants were asked to execute the task in Word 7.0 on a 66 MHz 80486 PC. They were all experienced in Word, and started with a blank Word document. They received the booklet with the experimental material. The experimenter read the introductory page with the participants, he explained the visual instructions and the experimental task. Afterwards, participants had to write their instruction without a time limit. After the task, they filled out the last page of the booklet.

DATA ANALYSIS

The experimental instructions for using the radio alarm, that is, the 26 verbal goal slots and the 16 visual action slots, as illustrated in Figure 2—were used as a tool in eliciting similar written instructions and hence in collecting referentially comparable data.

Clause Analysis

In a preliminary analysis, each clause was numbered and identified as a goal unit, action unit or extra unit. Goal and action units verbally express (part of) one of the 26 goal slots or 16 action slots respectively. Clauses were identified as extra elements if they were not triggered directly by the experimental instruction. Table 1, which records a participant's description of the instructions in Figure 2, illustrates this clause analysis: it contains four goal clauses, four action clauses and two extra (consequence) units.

Referential Analysis: Referring Expressions (NPs) and Identification Acts (Propositions)

In the referential analysis of the data, we restricted ourselves to the way in which participants introduced and reintroduced the most central discourse referents, the nine buttons (eight push, one switch) on the radio alarm. In view of the hypotheses mentioned previously, we defined and analyzed three subsets of referential data: (a) Set 1: a set of nine introductory NPs per subject, each of which is embedded in an action sentence in which this button is to be used for the first time in the radio alarm instructions; (b) Set 2: a set of preparatory propositional identification acts that precede the first occurrence of a button in an action sequence; (c) Set 3: a set of two anaphoric NPs per subject, that refer to instructive situations in which different subtasks have to be performed with a same single button.

These sets are defined on the basis of the experimental visual instructions that guarantee the comparability of the referential data in the different conditions. Furthermore, the sets are closely related to the dependent variables: each set offers a different interpretation of the notion of referential overspecification (perceptual,

TABLE 1
Analysis of a Text Fragment in Clauses, Slot Number, and Information Type (Dutch version with English glosses)

Text Fragments	*Slot Number*[a]	*Information Type*
Om de tijd in te stellen "To set the time"	1	goal
hou je **de meest linkse knop** ingedrukt "keep the leftmost button pressed"	1.1.1 + 1.1.2	action
Nu kan je het uur instellen. "Now you can set the hour"	1.1.1	goal
Om dat te doen "To do that"	1.1.1	goal
druk je op **de derde knop** "you press the third button"	1.1.1	action
tot je het gewenste uur bekomt "until you get the desired hour"	1.1.1	[conseq.]
Dan kan je de minuten instellen "Then you can set the minutes"	1.1.2	goal
Dat doe je door op **de vierde knop** te drukken "You do that by pressing the fourth button"	1.1.2	action
tot je het gewenste aantal minuten bekomt "until you obtain the desired minutes"	1.1.2	[conseq.]
Nu mag je **de meest linkse knop** loslaten. "Now you can let go of the leftmost button"	1.1.1 + 1.1.2	action

Note. Target Set 1 NPs are bold.
[a]See Figure 2.

propositional and anaphoric overspecification respectively) and Set 1 allows for an unambiguous definition of perception based as opposed to nonperception based NPs.

Set 1: Introductory NPs

Set 1 contains the nine NPs per subject, that refer to each of the nine buttons on the radio alarm and that occur in the first action sentence that refers to that button. Example (3), which verbalizes the first instructions given in Figure (2), contains two introductory NPs:

(3) To set the hour, keep pressing *the large square button on the left* and push *the small square button* repeatedly until you get the right result.

The NPs in this set are named introductory because—according to the visual instructions—they all refer to the first time a button is to be used in a radio alarm action. This, however, does not mean that these NPs are all first mention NPs in the text. In the instructive texts, the 'introductory' NPs in action sentences can be preceded by NPs in so-called preparatory propositional identification acts, as in (4); see Set 2). These are propositions in which the identification of an action button is prepared. As such, the definition of introductory NPs in Set 1 enables us to differentiate between two relevant referential strategies. First, writers can opt for the 'referential minimum', as in (3), and introduce the buttons directly in the action sentence. In that case the introductory NP in Set 1 is a non-anaphoric NP. Or, they can invest extra referential effort and prepare the action buttons in one or more identification acts preceding the action sentence, as in (4). In that case the introductory NP is anaphorically related to the NPs in these preparatory propositional identification acts.

(4) [Somewhere on your radio alarm, there have to be *two buttons, that enable you to set the hour*].
[In my case, it is *a large square* and *a small square button.*]
[In your case, it might be different].
[So you will have to look for *them.*]
[How do you know you have *the right button*?]
[If you press *the large one*, the hour display lights up].
[If you press *the small one*, the time on the display changes.]
To set the hour, keep pressing *the large square button on the left* and push *the small square button* more than once until you get the right result.

Perception based and nonperception based Set 1 NPs. According to the hypotheses, we are only interested in the dichotomy between perception based vs non-perception based NPs. Perception based NPs include perceptual characteristics triggered by the experimental instruction, in particular about the size (e.g., the *large* button), the shape (e.g., the *square* button) or the location of the object (e.g., the *left* button). Nonperception based NPs can take almost all relevant factors within the communicative setting as an anchor point, that is, the device, the user, the (ongoing) task, the instructor, the (ongoing) text. An illustrative survey of all these strategies is given in Appendix 1.

Perceptual overspecification. For perception based NPs, one type of overspecification can easily be defined, that is, perceptual overspecification. NPs that contain more perceptual ingredients than necessary for unique identification of the referent within the given perceptual task context (provided by the visual instruction), can be said to be overspecified. As an example, in the overspecified NP in (5) at least one ingredient is superfluous: there is only one large square button, and there is only one button on the left.

(5) Push the [large] [square] button [on the left]

Set 2: Preparatory Propositional Identification Acts

Set 2 consists of all propositional identification acts that are used to prepare the introduction of buttons in action units. These acts either relate to an *individual* button or to a *list* of buttons. *Individual acts*, including *individual antecedent NPs*, prepare specific buttons to be used in the subsequent action unit on the local level of discourse, as in (4) or (6). *List-like acts*, including *list-like antecedents*, refer to a series of buttons on a more global level of discourse, either the six buttons on top—as in (7)—the three buttons on the side or the nine buttons together. As such they serve as an advance organizer for a number of subsequent actions to come.

(6) To set the hour, look for *a large square button*. Press *the button*.
(7) On top, there are *six buttons: a large square*... . To set the hour, press *the large square button*.

In preparing the introduction of a button, writers can take the user, the instructor or the radio alarm as a focal point. The user oriented acts express different degrees of the writer's responsibility for the correct identification of the button. It ranges from nondirectives (such as the existential-be act "There should be button x.") over explorative acts, leaving the responsibility to the reader (such as "Look for button x") to clear strong directives (such as "Did you find x"). An illustrative survey of different types of acts is given in Appendix 2.

'Propositional' overspecification. The definition of set 2 enables us to define a second interpretation of referential overspecification that is a relevant determinant of the participants' referential behavior: the number and nature of the propositional identification acts preceding the NP-expression in the action sentences.

Set 3: Anaphoric NPs

Set 3 consists of a number of clear-cut anaphoric NPs referring to the buttons, again based on the visual instructions. In the 16 visual action slots, the nine buttons are addressed 20 times (nine of which constitute the data in set 1). In most cases, more than one button is involved in executing the same action, as it is the case in Figure 2. This creates a 'competing candidate' situation that often naturally blocks the use of attenuated anaphoric forms (especially pronouns). However, in two cases, one of which is illustrated in Figure 3, only one button is involved in two successive, related actions. In the two cases, almost all participants referred to the button in two successive action sentences or clauses within the same paragraph with no other references to competing buttons. These two cases result in (maximally) two anaphoric NPs per subject, which together constitute Set 3.

Anaphoric overspecification. Set 3 enables us to investigate the occurrence of overspecification as it is defined in theories like Accessibility or Givenness. Within

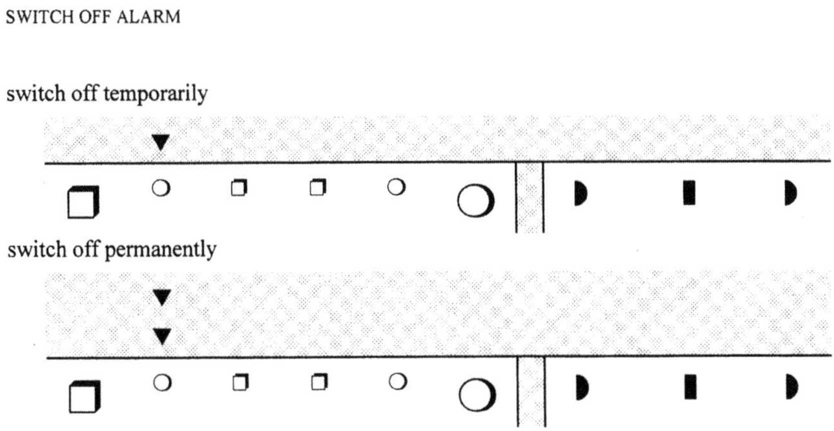

FIGURE 3 Sample of a visual instruction that triggers anaphoric reference

this line of thought, NP-types that mark low accessibility but refer to highly accessible referents, can be said to be overspecified. The anaphoric NPs in Set 3 are assumed to refer to highly activated referents on the basis of two standard textual variables: referential distance and competing candidates. There is no doubt that many other variables and variable types are responsible for the (non-)activation of referents, but for current purposes it is sufficient to establish that, according to all standard interpretations of referential coherence, a referent is highly accessible if it occurs in subsequent clauses or sentences in which no other competing referent is mentioned.

In the anaphoric NPs in Set 3, three increasing and implicating levels of anaphoric overspecification can be distinguished. All nominal (nonpronominal) NPs (e.g., *the button, this button*) can be said to be anaphorically overspecified, as they all do more than the bare minimum, that is, provide more information than necessary; a (demonstrative) pronoun already provides sufficient information. A second level of anaphoric overspecification applies if these nominal NPs consist of more than a simple determiner and noun, that is, if they contain attributive (in this case almost exclusively perceptual) elements (e.g., *this left button*). Finally, a third level of overspecification applies to so-called uniquely identifying NPs, that is, anaphoric NPs that contain enough lexical information (nouns and attributes) for unique identification of referents independent of the preceding linguistic context.

RESULTS

In this section, we present the results of the three data sets in the different conditions in relation to the hypotheses. Unless otherwise stated, the data were analyzed by means of a 2 × 2 analysis of variance, with visual identity (same vs. different) and reader's goal (do vs. learn) as factors.

Set 1: Perception Based NPs and Perceptual Overspecification

Table 2 presents the results of Set 1, that is, the set of nine NPs per subject that refer to the first occurrence of each button in the visual instructions. The first row represents the mean number of Set 1-NPs realized per subject. It shows that the setup of the production experiment produces fairly complete data: participants to a large extent verbalized or realized the nine introductions of the buttons in the appropriate action sentences. Participants in the VD condition are less explicit than participants in the VS condition $F(1, 101) = 15.15, p < .001$, probably because VD writers conceptualize their task differently. They know that their assumed readers have to apply the actions onto a device that is functionally identical indeed, but perceptually completely different. Therefore, they allow themselves more latitude in describing the specific, device-oriented actions and they do not always follow the visual instructions literally.

Apart from that, writers in the LEARN condition are more complete than DO writers $F(1, 101) = 4.75$, $p < .05$. Apparently, the assumed learning task incites writers to describe the actions more completely, a result that is consistent with the observation that the participants in the learn condition on average produce longer instructive texts (VS DO: 433 words; VS LEARN: 481; VD DO: 476, VD LEARN 521). There was no interaction ($F<1$).

Perception based NPs. The mean number of perception based NPs per subject in Table 2 shows the pervasive influence of the assumed physical identity of the device on the way in which writers conceptualize the objects to be located and identified. The difference between the VS and VD conditions is significant

TABLE 2
Set 1: Mean Number of Realized NPs , Perception Based NPs, and Perceptually Overspecified NPs (Without and With Antecedent) per Subject (Max. No = 9)

	Visually Same (VS)		*Visually Different (VD)*	
	Do	*Learn*	*Do*	*Learn*
NPs realized	8.70	8.95	7.72	8.36
Perception based NPs	8.15	7.19	0.86	2.36
Perceptually overspecified NPs	3.59	4.76	0.07	0.50
Perception based NPs preceded by antecedent in identification act	1.48	1.14	0.38	0.46
Perceptually overspecified NPs preceded by antecedent in identification act	0.44	0.43	0.03	0.07

$F(1, 101) = 151.46$, $p < .001$. Writers in the VS condition produce almost exclusively references based on the perceptual characteristics of the buttons—that is, on their size, shape, and position. Conversely, in the VD condition, the use of perception based descriptions is low.

The use of perception based expressions in the VS condition may not be surprising, as the device provides the writer with a straightforward and robust means of conceptualizing the protagonist objects. Still, especially in the VS-LEARN condition, in which writers work toward a meaningful and lasting description of the radio alarm instructions, one may expect writers to use more user and task oriented, functional descriptions (e.g., *the alarm button*) than in de VS-DO condition, at least as an addition to the basic perception based strategy. But the difference between DO and LEARN is negligible $F(1, 101) = 1.77$, *ns*, which disconfirms our hypothesis on this point.

In the VD condition, buttons are referred to by a large variety of nonperception based expressions, as they are illustrated in Appendix 1. The use of perception based descriptions in the VD condition is restricted to a small number of participants, who consistently opted for perceptual references (3 DO participants, 8 LEARN participants, resulting in an interaction between visual identity and goal, $F(1, 101) = 6.20$, $p < .05$. Except for one participant in the DO condition, they all motivate this perceptual strategy by explicitly stating in the introduction that they take their own device as a starting point, knowing that their assumed reader will have to 'transfer' the instructions to their own situation. Thus, these writers deliberately pass the responsibility onto the reader. This strategy may be seen as a simple emanation of the writer's laziness, that is, as an easy way of coming to grips with the complex writing task. On the other hand, transferring and applying instructions within a new or different situational setting can be seen as a powerful advanced way of learning. Within theories of skill learning like Anderson's (1983) ACT* model, these activities naturally fit in with the final, so-called autonomous learning phase. Within this perspective, the large number of LEARN-participants using this strategy (8 participants) may be relevant, given the nature of the assumed task they focus on and the long-term importance of the task that may justify writers to use a demanding referential strategy like this one.

Perceptual overspecification. The third row in Table 2 shows the mean number of perception based Set1-NPs that are perceptually overspecified. Evidently, perceptually overspecified NPs are more frequent in the VS condition than in the VD condition $F(1, 101) = 123.01$, $p < .001$, due to the near absence of perception based NPs in the VD-condition. In the VS condition, about half of all NPs is perceptually overspecified, that is, contains more perceptual ingredients than necessary to unambiguously locate and identify the button involved (3.59 and 4.76). Although the data do not provide us with an independent yard stick, this can be considered a large proportion.

If we look at perception based NPs that are preceded by an antecedent embedded in a preparatory propositional identification act (see set 2), and that are perceptually overspecified, the mean number of "overspecified NPs" understandably decreases, but still remains considerable (DO: .44 of 1.48; LEARN: .43 of 1.14).

Writers in the LEARN condition produce significantly more "overspecified NPs" than writers in the DO condition $F(1, 101) = 5.20, p < .05$. There was no interaction $F(1, 101) = 1.11, p = .30$.

Set 2: Propositional Overspecification

Table 3 shows the degree of *propositional overspecification* in the different conditions, defined as the mean number of preparatory propositional identification acts per (Set 2). Participants in the VS condition produce between 1 and 2 identification acts, VD participants more than 6. This difference is significant $F(1, 101) = 42.52$, $p < .001$. This again shows the pervasive influence of the visual context. There was no main effect of goal nor an interaction (F's < 1). For VD writers, the high number of identification acts can be seen as a way of tackling the referential complexity of the instructor's task. If writers cannot rely on the physical identity of the device on the part of the user, they apparently are incited to extensively prepare the identification of the referents, a strategy that is almost absent if users are assumed to have the device at their disposal.

The same phenomenon can be observed in a more detailed way and from a different angle, by combining Set 1 and Set 2 and by looking at the mean number of Set1-NPs that are preceded by one or more individual or list-like antecedent(s) embedded in preparatory propositional identification acts (Set 2). Table 4 shows that Set1-NPs in the VD condition are more often preceded by an identification act than in the VS condition $F(1, 101) = 9.18, p < .01$. Individual acts predominantly occur in the VD condition $F(1, 101) = 60.30, p < .001$, whereas list-like acts are more frequent in the VS condition $F(1, 101) = 3.44, p < .05$ one tail. The preference for list-like acts in the VS condition is probably caused by the device: the row of buttons incites writers to describe the set of buttons as a whole. An exception is the relatively frequent

TABLE 3
Set 2: Mean Number of Preparatory Propositional Identification Acts per

	Visually Same (VS)		*Visually Different (VD)*	
	Do	*Learn*	*Do*	*Learn*
Mean number of preparatory propositional identification acts	1.52	1.10	6.52	6.32

TABLE 4
Set 1 & Set 2: Mean Number of Set1—NPs Preceded by an (Individual or List-like) Identification Act

	Visually Same (VS)		*Visually Different (VD)*	
	Do	*Learn*	*Do*	*Learn*
With preceding identification act	1.97	2.62	4.31	4.08
Individual act	0.30	0.19	4.07	2.29
List-like act	1.67	2.43	0.24	1.79

use of list-like acts in the VD-LEARN condition (1.79), which clearly cannot be triggered by the visual context. Rather speculatively, they may be seen as an advance-organizational tool, intended to stage the writer's instruction and the reader's task, a strategy that can be assumed to be more beneficial for learning readers, as they are supposed to understand and recall the whole procedure for future use.

Set 3: Anaphoric Overspecification

Table 5 presents the results of Set 3, and shows the mean number of realized anaphoric NPs, and the mean number of different subtypes of anaphoric NPs related to the different levels of anaphoric overspecification defined. As in Set 1, participants in the VD condition are less complete than participants in the VS condition $F(1, 101) = 4.04, p < .05$ and writers in the LEARN condition are more complete than DO writers $F(1, 101) = 14.11, p < .001$. The effect of visual identity is mainly due to the DO condition, but the interaction is not significant $F(1, 101) = 2.48, p = .12$.

The next rows in Table 5 show the distribution of different types of anaphoric NPs. Anaphors are either pronominal (row 2) or nominal (row 3). If they are nomi-

TABLE 5
Set 3: Mean Number of Realized Anaphoric NPs, Anaphorically Overspecified NPs (Max No = 2)

	Visually Same (VS)		*Visually Different (VD)*	
	Do	*Learn*	*Do*	*Learn*
Anaphoric NPs realized	1.67	1.90	1.28	1.86
Pronominal anaphors	0.23	0	0.25	0.15
Nominal anaphors (level 1)	1.44	1.90	1.03	1.71
Attributive nominal anaphors (level 2)	0.93	1.48	0.76	1.18
Uniquely identifying nominal anaphors (level 3)	0.48	1.05	0.31	0.32

nal, they can be 'bare,' that is, a definite or demonstrative determiner plus noun (e.g., *the/this button*), or they can be amended with an attribute (row 4) (e.g., *the/this small button*). And if they are attributive, these attributes can be enough to uniquely identify the intended button (row 5).

The results in Table 5 show a large proportion of anaphoric overspecification on the three levels defined. First, nominal anaphors (level 1 overspecification) outnumber pronominals, although almost all Set2-NPs can be replaced naturally by a simple (unmarked or marked) pronominal, and the eliciting visual instructions (a same and single button in successive subactions) suggest an attenuated referential form. This level 1 overspecification may be explained partly by two characteristics that are not specific to the instructive context. First, in most cases, the Set 2 anaphors are used in second-mention position, a position in which the referent can be regarded to be not fully established yet. This validates the use of nominal NPs, as is observed in the results of other production experiments (e.g., Maes, 1997). Second, the referents involved are inanimate (buttons), and inanimate referents are less naturally referred to by pronouns than animates, as is argued for in Fraurud (1996) and Maes (1997).

But even if we would judge the overwhelming use of nominal anaphors to be natural, it would not explain the two other levels of anaphoric overspecification displayed. A considerable number of the nominal anaphors contains attributive elements (Level 2 overspecification), and a considerable number of these anaphors contain enough attributes to enable readers to uniquely identify the intended buttons (Level 3 overspecification).

Apart from these overall large portions of overspecification, the means differ over the different conditions. Nominal anaphors are more frequent in the LEARN and VS condition compared to the DO and VD condition (LEARN vs DO: $F(1, 101) = 22.82$, $p < .001$; VS vs. VD: $F(1, 101) = 6.33, p < .05$). There was no interaction ($F < 1$). Attributive anaphors are more frequent in the LEARN condition (LEARN vs DO: $F(1, 101) = 10.15, p < .01$; VS vs. VD: $F(1, 101) = 2.33, p = .13$). There was no interaction ($F < 1$). Uniquely identifying anaphors are more frequent in the LEARN and VS condition compared to the DO and VD condition (LEARN vs DO: $F(1, 101) = 4.72, p < .05$; VS vs. VD: $F(1, 101) = 11.42, p < .01$; interaction $F(1, 101) = 4.37, p < .05$.

In sum, the results show that the visual identity of the device and the assumed goal of the reader lead to the production of anaphorically overspecified NPs and incite participants to rely more on the direct, exophoric referential procedure even in textual conditions that normally trigger a text based endophoric referential strategy.

CONCLUSIONS

The results of the production experiment confirm the role of the two language-in-use factors in introducing and maintaining referents within an instructive context. The visual identity of the device largely determines the referential strategies used; *visually same* referents are introduced and reintroduced fairly systematically by means of perceptually overspecified NPs. Apart from that, writers show a number of referential strategies that fit in with the assumed goal on the part of their reader. These results enable us to draw a number of conclusions on the functional interpretation of referential expressions that are not so much based on the assumed activation of underlying discourse referents, but rather on the strategic writers' anticipation of the readers' behavior within a situational context that closely integrates text and task.

Visual Presence and Overspecification

Both in introducing referents and in anaphorically referring to referents, instructive writers to a large extent produce perceptually overspecified expressions. The size of the perceptual overspecification in the VS condition is striking, especially when we take into account the relative simplicity of the perceptual features of the referents and of the actions to be performed. This overspecification cannot be the result of the incremental nature of constructing adequate referential expressions, as Pechmann (1989) explained the overspecification in his data, because the experimental task aimed at producing well-considered informal written discourse. Apparently, instructive writers tend to use overspecified expressions not only as an emergency procedure, but also as a deliberate strategy.

This strategy can be related to the principle of distant responsibility proposed by Clark & Wilkes-Gibbs (1986), which explains extra efforts of language users in a nonfeedback situation. In this case, this may mean that the instructive writers consider the production of more identification information as more responsible and cooperative behavior. This idea is not unproblematic, however, as we know that overspecified expressions can be misleading especially in retrieving highly activated referents, because they violate normal expectations about attention allocation. Still, specific conditions in instructive discourse apparently overrule these expectations. The first condition is the obligation to perceptually identify and locate referents in instructions, which may account for the frequent use of extra perception information in referring to visually same referents. Given the importance of location and perception, each perceptual cue can be seen as 'affording information' that enables readers to bridge the gap between instruction and action, an idea that is in line with the arguments given in Glenberg & Robertson (1999). The second condition is the close integration of text and task, which results in the fragmentation of the process of reading instructions. Reading instructions has to be alternated with executing actions. Especially the use of the uniquely identifying (Level 3) anaphors in Set 3 is likely to be related to this switching behavior. These anaphors are unusual given the high activation status of their referents. Yet, they become highly efficient for a reader who is forced to constantly switch between text and task, as they contain enough perceptual information to unambiguously identify the intended button, which allows readers to use the 'direct' exophoric referential procedure instead of the 'indirect,' text based one.

In sum, perceptually overspecified expressions can be seen as reflecting the writer's awareness of the situational conditions in which instructive discourse is used.

The Assumed Goal of the Reader and Overspecification

Also, the assumed reader's goal has an impact on the production of overspecified expressions. A number of writers' strategies show the relevance of the difference between learning and doing, and hence the sensitivity of writers to the reader's goal. First, there is an association between learning and more information, which is reasonable as the task for the learner is judged to be more important; hence writers feel more distantly responsible and produce more information. Second, learning is associated with more perceptual and anaphoric overspecification, which again stresses the importance of perceptual information, not only in directly executing actions, but also in learning procedures. Unexpectedly, writers in the learn condition did not produce more functional descriptions, despite the evidence for an association between learning and functional, explanatory information (Kieras & Bovair, 1984; Ummelen, 1997). Perhaps the task was overall too simple for writers in the learn condition to engage in more explanatory referential behavior.

Furthermore, individual writers in the learn condition show strategies that fit in with this goal: a number of writers in the VD-learn condition use a writer-centered identification strategy that completely leaves the task to the readers and incites them to invest in transferring and applying the task onto their own situation. This fits in with the advanced idea of learning by transferring and applying information in a new situation. Also, they use much more list-like advance-organizing identification acts, which are capable of looking ahead at the writer's instruction and the reader's task.

Visual Identity and the Importance of Spatial Information

If perceptual information is relevant to the reader, as in the *visually same* condition, instructive writers massively opt for perceptual descriptions, both in introducing referents (Set 1) and in anaphorically referring to them (Set 3). And even if the perceptual context of the reader is unknown, as in the *visually different* condition, some instructive writers take their own perceptual context as a referential anchor point. Undoubtedly, this perceptual referential strategy is simply convenient and easy for instructive writers. But if it were to serve only their own convenience, one might expect that writers in both conditions would equally opt for it, which is not the case. So, the preference for perceptual information in the VS condition is likely to show the writers' awareness of the conditions in which readers use the instructions. Furthermore, the results show the writers' assessment of the important role of spatial-perceptual information for users of instructive discourse and, hence, add to the growing evidence on the crucial role of spatial information in constructing mental representations.

The importance of spatial information is convincingly argued for in relation with narrative discourse. Following earlier experiments on the role of protagonists in narrative text comprehension (Morrow, 1985), Morrow and his colleagues carried out a number of experiments that pointed out that during narrative text comprehension, the spatial information associated with protagonists is more accessible than other (spatial) information (e.g., Morrow, Greenspan, & Bower, 1987; Wilson, Rinck, McNamara, Bower, & Morrow, 1993). They concluded that narrative readers build a spatial model of the situation described and use that model to highlight information associated with the protagonist of the narrative. In their experiments, they used a prememorized map that artificially focused readers on spatial information during reading. Later experiments (e.g., De Vega, 1995; Hakala, 1999; O'Brien & Albrecht, 1992) indicated that spatial information is not automatically available during comprehension, but only if readers were asked to focus on spatial details, or if spatial information was a necessary precondition for text comprehension.

A drawback of these experiments is that they lack a natural communicative context: asking participants to focus on spatial information or to prememorize maps in relation to narrative texts, does not really meet natural reader's goals and functional reading conditions. In this experiment, on the other hand, the task as well as the availability of spatial information are realistic and represent the communicative act of informally instructing distant readers. This task becomes more and more natural as the digital evolution facilitates quick and interactive written message modes (such as e-mail, chat or discussion fora), and as the number of products, features and functions which require instructive information explosively increases. So, if writers in these conditions largely opt for spatial referential strategies, knowing that they have other strategies readily available as well, it can be seen as indirect evidence for the crucial role of spatial information in building mental representations of instructions, given our claim that the writers' referential strategies anticipate the readers' cognitive needs.

Visual Difference and Propositional Overspecification

If instructors cannot rely on a shared visual situation, they systematically opt for the production of preparatory propositional identification acts. This strategy can not be explained by characteristics of the communication mode used, as Cohen (1984) did for similar phenomena in his spoken corpus of instructions. Rather, it reflects the more complex writers' task in the *visually different* condition. The complexity was not caused by the fact that VD writers had to visually reconstruct the radio alarm, because the uncertainty about the perceptual characteristics of the toy bear shaped radio alarm made this useless; neither because of the unavailability of appropriate descriptions, as for each button a clear and unambiguous functional description was available (alarm button, snooze button, etc.). Rather, the preparatory acts aimed at establishing common ground about the spatial situation of actions, and expressed different methods to locate and identify the intended referents. Once again, the use of these identification acts shows the writers' sensitivity to the conditions in which readers have to use the instructions.

In sum, the overwhelming bias of perception as a source of conceptualizing referents is congruent with results obtained in Glenberg and Robertson (1999). Perception is considered a sound and straightforward way of conceptualizing referents. Still, it is surprising that other identification sources are so much suppressed, given the preference for functional descriptions in everyday instructions for use.

Overspecified Expressions and the Mental Activation of Referents

The results of this article contribute to our understanding of overspecified referential expressions in discourse. It is generally assumed that there is a relationship between the types of referential expressions and the degree of activation of discourse referents. The less activated a referent is, the more informative the referential expression has to be. In this framework, overspecified referential expressions are explained in terms of the conditions that affect the availability of the referents. These results have been obtained mainly in narrative and expository texts. The results of this experiment do not falsify this theory, but they suggest that it needs to be expanded so as to comprise other factors than the activation level of referents, if one wants to account for reference maintenance in other discourse genres as well.

This study with instructive texts demonstrated an overwhelming occurrence of overspecified referential expressions. The two task-induced factors used in the experiment affect the type of overspecification produced: the visually same condition and the learning goal condition increase both the number of perceptually overspecified expressions and the number of anaphorically overspecified expressions. The visually different condition increases the number of propositionally overspecified expressions.

The overspecification results can be interpreted in terms of the distant responsibility of the instructive writers. In anticipating the reader's task, they produce an excess of information to minimize the risk that the reader cannot perform the task. The *type* of overspecification depends on the specific conditions. Given the nature of the instructions (manipulating concrete objects in a physical task context), the use of spatial representations is obviously beneficial, and, accordingly, there is a preference for perceptually overspecified expressions. This tendency increases when the writer assumes visually identical referents to be used by the reader and when the reader's goal is more critical (learning as opposed to doing). If no identical referents are present for the assumed reader, the type of overspecifications changes from perceptual overspecification into propositional overspecification.

REFERENCES

Almor, A. (1999). Noun-phrase anaphora and focus: The informational load hypothesis. *Psychological Review, 106*, 748–765.

Anderson, J. R. (1983). *The architecture of cognition*. Cambridge, MA: Harvard University Press.

Anderson, A., Garrod, S. C., & Sanford, A. J. (1983). The accessibility of pronominal antecedents as a function of episode shifts in narrative text. *Quarterly Journal of Experimental Psychology, 35*, 427–440.

Ariel, M. (1988). Referring and accessibility. *Journal of Linguistics, 24*, 65–87.

Ariel, M. (1990). *Accessing noun-phrase antecedents*. London: Routledge.

Beun, R. J., & Cremers, A. H. M. (1998). Object reference in a shared domain of conversation. *Pragmatics & Cognition, 6*, 121–152.

Carreiras, M., & Gernsbacher, M. A. (1992). Comprehending conceptual anaphors in Spanish. *Language and Cognitive Processes, 7*, 281–299.

Chapanis, A., Parrish, R. N., Ochsman, R. B., & Weeks, G. D. (1977). Studies in interactive communication II. The effects of four communication modes on the linguistic performance of teams during cooperative problem solving. *Human Factors, 19*, 101–125.

Clark, H. H., & Wilkes-Gibbs, D. (1986). Referring as a collaborative process. *Cognition, 22*, 1–39.

Cohen, P. R. (1984). The pragmatics of referring and the modality of communication. *Computational Linguistics, 10*, 97–146.

De Vega, M. (1995). Backward updating of mental models during continuous reading of narratives. *Journal of Experimental Psychology: Learning, Memory & Cognition, 25*, 373–385.

Fletcher, C. R. (1984). Markedness and topic continuity in discourse processing. *Journal of Verbal Learning and Verbal Behavior, 23*, 487–493.

Francik, E. P. (1985). *Referential choice and focus of attention in narratives*. Unpublished doctoral dissertation, Stanford University, Connecticut.

Fraurud, K. (1996). Cognitive ontology and NP form. In T. Fretheim & J. K. Gundel (Eds.), *Reference and referent accessibility* (pp. 65–87). Amsterdam: Benjamins.

Garrod, S., Freudenthal, D., & Boyle, E. (1994). The role of different types of anaphor in the on-line resolution of sentences in discourse. *Journal of Memory and Language, 33*, 39–68.

Gernsbacher, M. A., & Hargreaves, D. (1988). Accessing sentence participants: The advantage of first mention. *Journal of Memory and Language, 27*, 699–717.

Glenberg, A. M., & Robertson, D. A. (1999). Indexical understanding of instructions. *Discourse Processes, 28*, 1–26.

Gordon, P. C., Grosz, B. J., & Gilliom, L. A. (1993). Pronouns, names, and centering of attention in discourse. *Cognitive Science, 17*, 311–347.

Gordon, P. C., & Hendrick, R. (1997). Intuitive knowledge of linguistic co-reference. *Cognition, 62*, 325–370.

Gordon, P. C., Hendrick, R., Ledoux, K., & Yang, C. L. (1999). Processing of reference and the structure of language: An analysis of complex noun phrases. *Language and Cognitive Processes, 14*, 353–379.

Grosz, B. J., Joshi, A. K., & Weinstein, S. (1995). Centering: A framework for modelling the local coherence of discourse. *Computational Linguistics, 21*, 203–225.

Gundel, J. K., Hedberg, N., & Zacharski, R. (1993). Cognitive status and the form of referring expressions in discourse. *Language, 69*, 274–307.

Hakala, C. M. (1999). Accessibility of spatial information in a situation model. *Discourse Processes, 27*, 261–279.

Jansen, C., & Maes, A. (1999). Document Design. *South African Journal of Linguistics, 17*, 234–255.

Kieras, D. E., & Bovair, S. (1984). The role of a mental model in learning to operate a device. *Cognitive Science, 8*, 341–371.

Klein, W. (1982). Deixis and spatial orientation in route directions. In R. J. Jarvella & W. Klein (Eds.). *Speech, place and action. Studies in deixis and related topics*, (pp. 283–311). Chichester, England: Wiley.

Krauss, R. M., & Weinheimer, S. (1966). Concurrent feedback, confirmation and the encoding of referents in verbal interaction. *Journal of Personality and Social Psychology, 4*, 343–346.

Maes, A. (1991). An institutional view on discourse reference. *Gramma. Tijdschrift voor Taalkunde, 15*, 23–55.

Maes, A. (1997) Referent ontology and centering in discourse. *Journal of Semantics, 14*, 207–235.

Maes, A. (2000). What can production data teach us about the effectiveness of instructive text design variables? *Document Design, 1*, 170–181.

Maes, A., & Lenting, H. (1999). How to put the instructive space into words? *IEEE Transactions on Professional Communication, 42*, 100–113.

Maes, A., & Noordman, L. G. M. (1995). Demonstrative nominal anaphors: A case of non-identificational markedness. *Linguistics, 33*, 255–282.

Marcus, N., Cooper, M., & Sweller, J. (1996). Understanding instructions. *Journal of Educational Psychology, 88*, 49–63.

Marlsen-Wilson, W., & Levy, E. (1982). Producing interpretable discourse: The establishment and maintenance of reference. In R. J. Jarvella & W. Klein (Eds.), *Speech, place and action. Studies in deixis and related topics* (pp. 339–378). Chichester, England: Wiley.

Mayer, R. E., Bove, W., Bryman, A., Mars, R., & Tapango, L. (1996). When less is more: Meaningful learning from visual and verbal summaries of science textbook lessons. *Journal of Educational Psychology, 88*, 64–73.

Morrow, D. G. (1985). Prominent characters and events organize narrative understanding. *Journal of Verbal Learning and Verbal Behavior, 24*, 304–319.

Morrow, D. G., Greenspan, S. L., & Bower, G. H. (1987). Accessibility and situational models in narrative comprehension. *Journal of Memory and Language, 26*, 165–187.

O'Brien, E. J., & Albrecht, J. E. (1992) Comprehension strategies in the development of a mental model. *Journal of Experimental Psychology: Learning, Memory and Cognition, 18*, 777–784.

Pechmann, T. (1989). Incremental speech production and referential overspecification. *Linguistics, 27*, 89–110.

Schober, M. F. (1993). Spatial perspective-taking in conversation. *Cognition, 47*, 1–24.

Schober, M. F. (1995). Speakers, addressees, and frames of reference: Whose effort is minimized in conversations about locations? *Discourse Processes, 20*, 219–247.

Smith, E. E., & Goodman, L. (1984). Understanding written instructions: The role of explanatory schema. *Cognition and Instruction, 1*, 359–396.

Ummelen, N. (1997). *Procedural and declarative information in software manuals. Effects on information use, task performance and knowledge*. Amsterdam: Rodopi.

von Stutterheim, C., & Kohlmann, U. (1998). Selective hearer-adaptation. *Linguistics, 36*, 517–549.

Vonk, W., Hustinx, L., & Simons, W. (1992). The use of referential expressions in structuring discourse. *Language and Cognitive Processes, 7*, 301–333.

Ward, G., Sproat, R., & McKoon, G. (1991). A pragmatic analysis of so-called anaphoric islands. *Language, 67*, 439–474.

Wilson, S., Rinck, M., McNamara, T. P., Bower, G. H., & Morrow, D. G. (1993). Mental models and narrative comprehension: Some qualifications. *Journal of Memory and Language, 32*, 141–154.

Wright, P. (1990). Using constraints and reference in task-oriented dialogue. *Journal of Semantics, 7,* 65–79.

Yule, G., & Powers, M. (1994). Investigating the communicative outcomes of task-based interaction. *System, 22,* 81–91.

APPENDIX 1
NP Analysis: Different Ways of Conceptualizing Buttons

device-oriented ingredients

–perception	
–the size of the object	**the *large* button**
–the shape of the object	**the *square* button**
–the location of the object	**the *left* button**
–the semantics of the object (the presence of which is often a syntactic necessity as it provides the NP with the necessary head noun)	**the *button***
–system characteristics of the object	**the button *with three positions***
–comparison with other objects	**a button *just like the time button***

user/task-based

–the function of the object	**the *alarm* button; the button *that indicates the alarm***
–the functional task users have to perform	**the button *that allows you to install the alarm***
–the 'functional location' of the object	**the button *with 'alarm' or 'al' on it***
–the action to be executed with the object	**the button *that you can put in three positions***
–the course of the task of the user	**the button *you did not have to use yet***

instructor-based

–reference to the instructor's ongoing task	**the button *I did not mention yet***
–naming or labeling of objects	**the button *I will refer to as B1***

text-based

–anaphoric link with an antecedent	***it; this button, the button***
–the course of the text	**(two buttons); *one... the other***

knowledge based

–assumed experience of the reader	**the button that is *usually* the largest one**

vague	**the *right/correct* button, *a button*, a *different* button.**

APPENDIX 2:
Identification Act Analysis:
Types of Preparatory Propositional Identification Acts

user/task oriented acts	
–existential be	**(In your case), there is (a list of) x**
–need-act	**You need x**
–search-act	**You should search/look for x**
–result-act	**Did you find x?**
–condition-act	**If you have found x, then..**
–control-act	**How do you know that you have the right button?**
–exploration-act	**Try A to find x.**
–task-oriented act	**is the only one that you did not have to use yet.**
instructor oriented acts	
–existential	**In my case, there is x**
–labeling objects	**I will label it as x.**
–expression of writer's assumption	**I will assume that x is..**
–expression of writer's guess or uncertainty	**I do not know how/where x is.**
device oriented acts	
–perception-based acts	**x has the form of y, x looks like y, x has position y.**
–function-oriented act	**x has the function of y.**
–system-based acts	**x works as follows.**

DISCOURSE PROCESSES, *37*(2), 145–164

Managing Mental Representations During Narrative Comprehension

Morton Ann Gernsbacher
Department of Psychology
University of Wisconsin–Madison

Rachel R. W. Robertson
Department of Psychology
University of Wisconsin–Madison

Paola Palladino
Department of Psychology
University of Padova

Necia K. Werner
Department of Psychology
University of Wisconsin–Madison

Three experiments investigated how readers manage their mental representations during narrative comprehension. The first experiment investigated whether readers' access to their mental representations of the main character in a narrative becomes enhanced (producing a "benefit") when the character is rementioned; the first experiment also investigated whether readers' access to the main character in a narrative becomes weakened or interfered with (producing a "cost") when a new character is introduced. The purpose of the second experiment was to ensure that there was nothing unusually salient about the accessibility of names; thus, we assessed readers' access to an object associated with the main character rather than the character's name. Again, readers demonstrated increased accessibility to the main character when it was rementioned in the narrative, and readers demonstrated reduced accessibility to the main character when a new character was introduced. A third experiment com-

Correspondence and requests for reprints should be sent to Morton Ann Gernsbacher, Department of Psychology, University of Wisconsin–Madison, 1202 W. Johnson Street, Madison, WI 53706–1611. E-mail: MAGernsb@facstaff.wisc.edu

pared more-skilled and less-skilled readers' abilities to manage these mental representations during narrative comprehension. Findings were consistent with research suggesting that more-skilled readers are more skilled at attenuating interfering information (i.e., suppression). Data from all 3 experiments suggest that successful narrative comprehension involves managing mental representations of salient and often times interfering characters.

To successfully read and comprehend a story, readers must keep track of narrative details: Who is the main character? What does he or she look like? What is his or her role in the story? and so on. Moreover, most narratives are complex; they usually contain more than 1 episode, and more than one character participates in the events. The task of keeping track of an infinite number of characters, mannerisms, places, plots, and subplots seems daunting, yet most readers succeed effortlessly. How do readers accomplish this feat with relatively little exertion?

According to the Structure Building Framework (Gernsbacher, 1990, 1995, 1997b), comprehenders use two general cognitive processes to build mental representations (structures) of texts such as narratives. These two processes are mapping and *shifting*. Through the process of mapping, comprehenders build mental structures by mapping related information onto their representations of previously comprehended information. However, if the incoming information is less related, a comprehender will shift to build a new substructure. These two cognitive processes, mapping and shifting, are enabled by two cognitive mechanisms: enhancement and suppression. Enhancement and suppression contribute to building mental representations by modulating the activation of concepts; *enhancement* increases the activation of relevant concepts, and *suppression* decreases the activation of concepts deemed less relevant (Gernsbacher, 1991; Gernsbacher & Faust, 1991a, 1991b). In this article we shall demonstrate how these general cognitive processes and mechanisms allow comprehenders to keep track of who is doing what to whom when comprehending a narrative.

Intuition suggests that the more often a character is mentioned in a narrative, the more accessible that character will become. We shall present data in this article that support this intuition. Perhaps less intuitive is the prediction that when a new character is introduced in a narrative, comprehenders' mental access to a previously introduced character is weakened. Some data already support this prediction, indirectly. Dell, McKoon, and Ratcliff (1983) presented four-sentence texts; the first three following sentences are examples of the first three sentences of one of their texts:

A burglar surveyed the garage set back from the street.
Several milk bottles were piled at the curb.
The banker and her husband were on vacation.

Dell and colleagues (1983) manipulated the final, fourth sentence. In one condition, the character introduced in the first sentence (e.g., *a burglar)* was rementioned anaphorically in the fourth sentence, as in,

The criminal slipped away from the street lamp.

In another condition, the character introduced in the first sentence was not rementioned in the fourth sentence. The fourth sentences in this 'no remention' condition shared the same predicate as the fourth sentences in the 'remention' condition (e.g., *The criminal slipped away from the street lamp),* for example,

A cat slipped away from the street lamp.

One way to conceptualize this experimental design is that the main character (always introduced in the first sentence) was rementioned in one condition, but in the other condition (what Dell et al., 1983 considered the 'no anaphor' condition) a new character (e.g., *a cat)* was introduced. According to the Structure Building Framework, introducing a new character would be an instance when the incoming information is less related to the previous information, and the comprehender should shift to build a new substructure. After comprehenders have shifted to develop a new substructure, information represented in the previous substructure is less accessible. Therefore, the Structure Building Framework predicts that introducing a new character would interfere with comprehenders' access to a previously mentioned character. The data by Dell and colleagues supported this prediction.

Dell and colleagues (1983) measured accessibility of the main character using a probe verification task: Participants were shown a probe word and asked to verify rapidly and accurately whether the word had occurred in the text that they were currently reading. On experimental trials, the probe word was the name of the main character. In one experiment, Dell and colleagues presented the probe words at two points in the fourth sentence, illustrated by the following asterisk and caret.

*The *criminal slipped away from the ^street lamp.*
*A*cat slipped away from the^street lamp.*

The asterisk marks an early test point, before either the main character was rementioned anaphorically or a new character was introduced. The caret marks a late test point, a few words downstream after either the main character was rementioned anaphorically or a new character was introduced. Verification latencies for the main character (e.g., *burglar)* did not differ at the early test point; at the late test point, verification latencies were slower when a new character was introduced. These data could be interpreted as demonstrating that rementioning a character (even anaphorically) improves its accessibility in readers' mental representations. Or these data could be interpreted as demonstrating that introducing a new character interferes with the accessibility of a previously introduced character. Without a neutral baseline, we cannot be sure whether this effect is a benefit—for rementioning a main character—or a cost—for introducing a new character (cf. Long & de Ley, 2000; Nordlie, Dopkins, & Johnson, 2001). One of the main goals of the research presented here was to provide such a neutral condition and tease apart these two interpretations.

Similarly, data from Gernsbacher (1989), using single sentences, are somewhat ambiguous about whether rementioning a main character leads to a benefit (the main character is more accessible in comprehenders' mental representations) and introducing a new character leads to a cost (the main character is less accessible in comprehenders' mental representations). In Gernsbacher's (1989) experiment, participants read sentences such as,

Bill handed John some tickets to a concert but Bill took the tickets back immediately.

in which a main character *(Bill)* was rementioned. Or they read sentences such as,

Bill handed John some tickets to a concert but Mark took the tickets back immediately,

in which a new character *(Mark)* was introduced. Verification latencies to the main character before versus after the main character was rementioned or the new character was introduced, showed faster verification latencies when the main character was rementioned and hence, slower verification latencies when a new character was introduced. As with the study by Dell and colleagues (1983) we need a neutral condition to allow us to determine whether rementioning a main character leads to a benefit (the main character is more accessible in comprehenders' mental representations) and introducing a new character leads to a cost (the main character is less accessible in comprehenders' mental representations).

We report three experiments here. In all three experiments, we presented participants with a set of narratives; each narrative comprised three paragraphs. In the first paragraph of all of the experimental narratives, one main character was introduced, for example:

Grant checked the control panels of the spacecraft. All the systems were ready. Grant, in his red and white shiny suit, coordinating boots, and special receiver medallion, was equally ready for this next mission of discovery. Just as the spacecraft crossed the border into a new universe, the red light of danger started to flash on the control panel, and the alarm began to scream.

We manipulated three versions of the second paragraph. In one version, the main character from the first paragraph was rementioned in the second paragraph, for example:

> *Grant, being the well-trained and organized leader, remained calm and began searching the database for information. There was clearly another spaceship within a few light-years away. Grant prepared the computer system to initiate communication with the foreign beings.*

In a second version, the main character from the first paragraph was not rementioned in the second paragraph; instead, a new character was introduced in the second paragraph, for example:

> *Alexa, being the well-trained and organized leader, remained calm and began searching the database for information. There was clearly another spaceship within a few light-years away. Alexa prepared the computer system to initiate communication with the foreign beings.*

In a third version, neither the main character from the first paragraph was rementioned, nor was a new character introduced in the second paragraph, for example:

> *It was necessary to remain calm and begin searching the database for information. There was clearly another spaceship within a few light-years away. The next step was to prepare the computer system to initialize communication with the foreign beings.*

Then, all the narratives concluded with a final paragraph, which was not manipulated across versions and served simply to wrap up the narrative.

We used a probe verification task to assess the accessibility of the main character at two experimental test points: immediately after the first paragraph (the paragraph that introduced the main character), and immediately after the second paragraph (the paragraph that rementioned the main character, introduced a new character, or did neither). By measuring participants' speed and accuracy to verify the main character's name (as having occurred in the narrative) at the two test points, we could assess any change in accessibility of the main character. Across all three conditions, we could assess whether any change in accessibility was a benefit (the main character became more accessible in comprehenders' mental representations) or a cost (the main character became less accessible in comprehenders' mental representations), based on a neutral baseline.

In the second experiment, we wanted to rule out the possibility that any change in accessibility observed in the first experiment (costs or benefits) were at a lexical level rather than a more conceptual level. Therefore, for the second experiment we used as a probe word for the experimental narratives the name of an object that had been associated with the main character rather than the main character's name. In a third experiment, we investigated whether individual differences in comprehension skill influences the way comprehenders manage their mental representations.

EXPERIMENT 1

This first experiment examined how readers keep track of who is doing what to whom while reading a narrative. We expected a boost in accessibility when the main character was rementioned and a decrease in accessibility when a new character was introduced.

Method

Participants. Eighty undergraduates at the University of Wisconsin–Madison participated to earn extra-credit in an introductory psychology course. In all experiments reported here, participants were native American English speakers, and none participated in more than one experiment.

Materials and Procedure. Thirty-two experimental narratives were constructed, each containing three paragraphs. In the first paragraph, a main character was introduced in the first sentence and rementioned in the third sentence. The second and fourth sentences of the first paragraph made no mention of any character. The second paragraph was manipulated in three ways: In what we shall refer to as the *Remention* condition, the main character was rementioned in the first sentence of the second paragraph. In what we shall refer to as the *New* condition, a new character was introduced in the first sentence of the second paragraph. In what we shall refer to as the *Neither* condition, neither the main character was rementioned nor a new character was introduced in the first sentence of the second paragraph.

The characters' names were typical, American first names commonly ascribed to only one gender (e.g., names such as "Pat" were avoided). In each narrative the main character's and the new character's names were matched for perceived familiarity and length in letters and were opposite in gender. Of the experimental main characters, 16 were men and 16 were women.

We used a verification task to assess participants' access to the main character. Within the three paragraph narratives, participants were required to verify whether several probe words, each presented at a various point, had occurred in the narrative they were currently reading. Participants pressed a key labeled "Yes" or a key labeled "No" to indicate their response.

To balance the number of "yes" and "no" responses and the pattern of "yes" and "no" responses within each narrative, 16 filler narratives were created. Experimental and filler narratives were presented in a randomized fixed order. In addition, in each experimental narrative a filler test point was included at the end to avoid a predictable pattern of "yes" and "no" responses and to increase the number of "no" responses without increasing the number of narratives. An example experimental narrative along with its probe words is shown in Table 1.

Four material sets were formed. Across materials, each experimental narrative occurred an equal number of times in all four of its experimental conditions: *before*, when the main character's name was tested before the beginning of the second paragraph; and *remention*, *new*, and *neither*, when the main character's name was tested just after the second paragraph. Twenty participants were randomly assigned to each material set; thus, each participant was exposed to an experimental narrative in only one of its conditions.

Participants read instructions from a computer screen, which told them that the experiment involved reading several short narratives, and that their task was to read each narrative at a natural reading rate. To encourage general comprehension, after 12 of the narratives, participants were asked to write, for a maximum time of 15 sec, a short, one-line continuation of the narrative. Participants didn't know while reading each narrative which narratives they would be required to continue.

TABLE 1.
Example Experimental Narrative From Experiment 1

Introduction

Grant checked the control panels of the spacecraft. All the systems were ready. Grant, in his red and white shiny suit, coordinating boots, and special receiver medallion, was equally ready for this next mission of discovery. Just as the spacecraft crossed the border into a new universe, the red light of danger started to flash on the control panel, and the alarm began to scream.

Experimental Probe Word: GRANT [for before condition]; **HEATHER** [for after condition]

Remention condition

Grant, being the well-trained and organized leader, remained calm and began searching the database for information. There was clearly another spaceship within a few light-years away. Grant prepared the computer system to initiate communication with the foreign beings.

New Condition

Alexa, being the well-trained and organized leader, remained calm and began searching the database for information. There was clearly another spaceship within a few light-years away. Alexa prepared the computer system to initiate communication with the foreign beings.

Neither Condition

It was necessary to remain calm and begin searching the database for information. There was clearly another spaceship within a few light-years away. The next step was to prepare the computer system to initialize communication with the foreign beings.

Experimental Probe Word: ALEXA [for before condition]; **GRANT** [for after condition]

Conclusion

Alexa turned on the monitor. Their hail was being answered. Hopefully, they would be cooperative. Often times they were, but there was no guarantee.

Filler Probe Word: HEATHER [for before condition]; **ALEXA** [for after condition]

The experimental session began with general instructions, which contained two practice trials. Each experimental trial began when the participant, after seeing the word "READY?" in the center of the screen and concurrently hearing the word "READY?" through headphones, pressed the "Advance" key. When participants pressed the "Advance" key, the "READY?" message disappeared. Then each paragraph of each narrative appeared in the center of the screen. Participants read each paragraph at their own pace without any time limit. Participants indicated they were finished reading each paragraph by pressing the "Advance" key. Immediately after the first, second and third paragraphs, a probe word was presented. Participants were required to decide if that probe word had occurred in the narrative, by pressing the "Yes" or "No" key. During the entire experiment, participants were required to keep the index and middle fingers of the hand that they normally write with on the "Yes" and "No" keys.

The complete set of materials for Experiment 1 is available at *http://psych.wisc.edu/lang/materials/charsupnames.html.*

Results

Response times faster than 250 ms were excluded from analysis. An accuracy criterion was established at 62% correct for each type of probe *(before, remention, new, and neither);* 13% of the participants did not reach the criterion and were replaced. Analyses of variance (ANOVA) of the probe verification data were separately conducted on verification errors and verification latency for correct responses. ANOVAs for both dependent variables compared the four different conditions: *before*, *remention*, *new*, and *neither*. Two sets of ANOVAs were conducted; one considering participants as a random effect (which we notate as *F1)* and one considering the probe words as a random effect (which we notate as *F2).*

Verification latencies. A significant main effect was observed, $F1(3, 79) = 71.84, p < .001$, $F2(3, 31) = 62.60, p < .001$. As shown in Figure 1, participants' verification latencies to the main character's name were faster after reading a second paragraph in which the main character was rementioned ($M = 556$, $SE = 19$) than after reading a second paragraph in which neither the main character was rementioned nor a new character was introduced ($M = 654$, $SE = 23$), $F1(1, 79) = 41.34, p < .001$, $F2(1, 31) = 32.13, p < .001$. Comparing the data from these two conditions (verification latencies in the remention condition and verification latencies in the neither condition) allows us to gauge a statistically significant benefit: Rementioning the main character increased its accessibility. Thus, in answer to our first experimental question we observed that a character does become *more* accessible in comprehenders' mental representations after the character is rementioned.

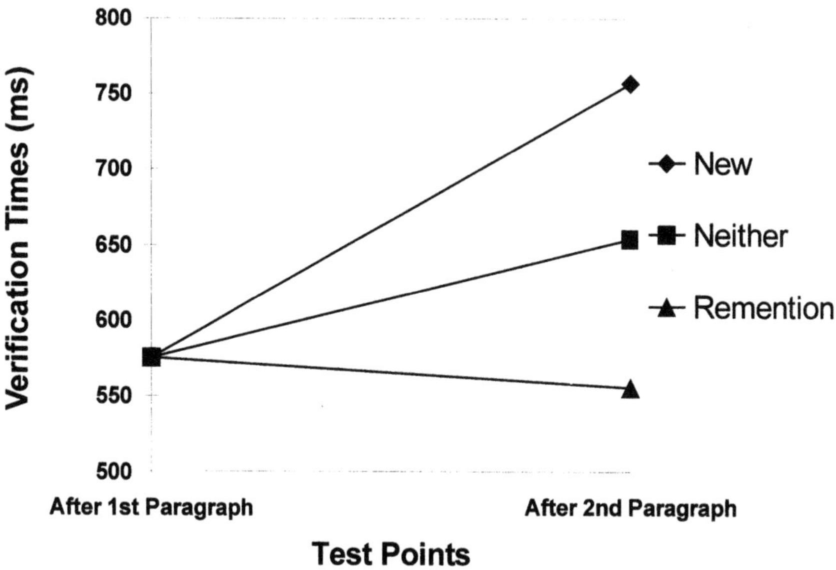

FIGURE 1 Participants' verification latencies (in ms) in Experiment 1.

Our second experimental question was whether a character becomes *less* accessible in comprehenders' mental representations after a new character is introduced. To answer this question we compared participants' verification latencies to the main character's name after reading a second paragraph in which a new character was introduced with their verification latencies to the main character's name after reading a second paragraph in which neither the main character was rementioned nor a new character was introduced. We observed that participants reaped a statistically significant cost: Introducing a new character interfered with the accessibility of an old character. As also shown in Figure 1, participants' verification latencies to the main character's name were slower after reading a second paragraph in which a new character was introduced ($M = 757$, $SE = 25$) than after reading a second paragraph in which neither the main character was rementioned nor a new character was introduced ($M = 654$, $SE = 23$), $F1(1, 79) = 45.58$, $p < .001$, $F2(1, 31) = 43.58$, $p < .001$. Participants' verification latencies to the main character's name were statistically equivalent before reading a second paragraph in which the main character was rementioned ($M = 575$, $SE = 22$) as after reading a second paragraph in which the main character was rementioned ($M = 556$, $SE = 19$).

Verification errors. As shown in Figure 2, the pattern from participants' verification errors was identical to that of their verification latencies. A significant main effect was observed, $F1(3, 79) = 40.36$, $p < .001$, $F2(3, 31) = 32.85$, $p < .001$.

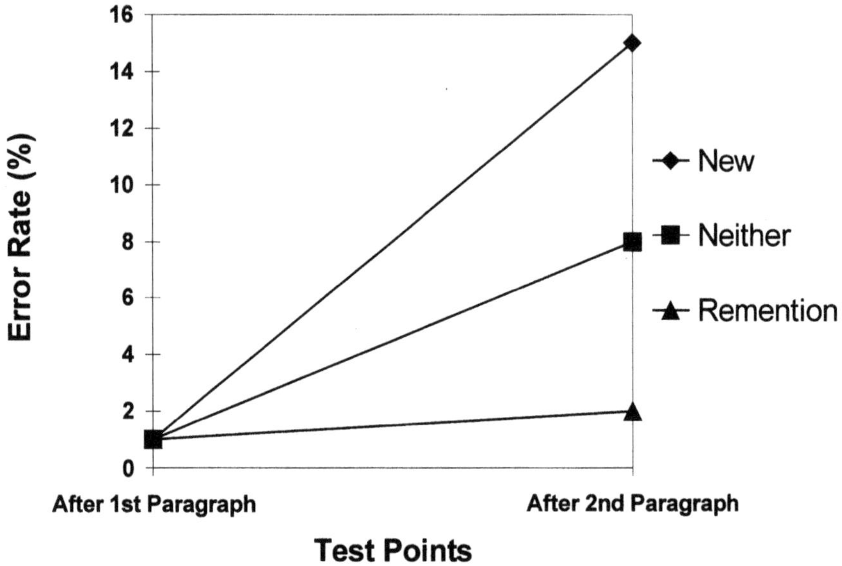

FIGURE 2 Participants' verification error rate (in percentage) in Experiment 1.

As with participants' verification latencies, participants' verification errors demonstrated a statistically significant benefit of rementioning a main character: Participants made fewer errors in verifying the main character's name after reading a second paragraph in which the main character was rementioned ($M = 2\%$, $SE = .6\%$) than after reading a second paragraph in which neither the main character was rementioned nor a new character was introduced ($M = 8\%$, $SE = 1.1\%$), $F1(1, 79) = 14.82$, $p < .001$, $F2(1, 31) = 12.22$, $p < .001$. And as with verification latencies, participants' verification errors demonstrated a statistically significant cost of introducing a new character: Participants made more errors when verifying the main character's name after reading a second paragraph in which a new character was introduced ($M = 15\%$, $SE = 1.8\%$) than after reading a second paragraph in which neither the main character was rementioned nor a new character was introduced ($M = 8\%$, $SE = 1.1\%$), $F1(1, 79) = 28.58$, $p < .001$, $F2(1, 31) = 23.57$, $p < .001$. As with verification latencies, participants' verification errors to the main character's name were statistically equivalent before reading a second paragraph in which the main character was rementioned ($M = 1\%$, $SE = .4\%$) as after reading a second paragraph in which the main character was rementioned ($M = 2\%$, $SE = .6\%$).

Discussion

The Structure Building Framework accounts for the results of Experiment 1 in the following way: When we read a narrative we have to keep track of who is doing what to whom. The first-mentioned character lays the mental foundation for the narrative and must be kept accessible to build a coherent text structure. According to the Structure Building Framework, a mapping process occurs during reading; through the process of mapping, related information is mapped on to previously comprehended information. When a previously introduced character is rementioned, he or she gains further accessibility by being mapped and further enhanced. However, if the incoming information is less related, a comprehender will shift to build a new substructure. When a new character is introduced, he or she is less related to the previous character, even if their syntactic and semantic features overlap. A new character interferes with the previous one, and readers must attenuate (i.e., suppress) the interference to focus on the new information and shift to build a new substructure.

EXPERIMENT 2

The goal of our second experiment was to further investigate the effects observed in our first experiment. In particular, we wanted to rule out the possibility that the results from Experiment 1 depended on a specific probe word (the character's name) rather than the readers' mental representation of that character (cf. Gordon, Hendrick, & Foster, 2000, who recently suggested caution in using probe verification tasks to assess anaphoric reference). Therefore, we wanted to extend the previous results by testing the accessibility of an object associated with the main character rather than the main character.

Method

Participants. Eighty-eight native American English speakers participated in this experiment; about half were members of Madison community who received a cash payment, and the other half were University of Wisconsin–Madison undergraduates who earned extra credit in an introductory psychology course.

Materials and procedure. The main difference between Experiment 1 and Experiment 2 was most prominently the probe words and less prominently the content of the narratives. The narratives used in Experiment 2 were slightly modified from those used in our first experiment to introduce an object and to express a relation between that object and the main character. An example experimental narrative along with its probe words is shown in Table 2. All probe words, even filler probe words were object names rather than character names.

All procedures remained identical to those outlined in Experiment 1. The complete set of materials for Experiment 2 can be found at http://psych.wisc.edu/lang/materials/charsupnouns.html.

TABLE 2
Example Experimental Narrative From Experiment 2

Introduction

Grant entered some numbers into the portable keypad attached to his wrist and then began to check the control panels of the spacecraft. All the systems were ready. Grant was equally ready for this next mission of discovery. Just as the spacecraft crossed the border into a new universe, the red light of danger started to flash on the control panel, and the alarm began to scream.

Experimental Probe Word: KEYPAD [for before condition]; **LASER** [for after condition]

Remention Condition

Grant, being the well-trained and organized leader, remained calm and began searching the database for information. There was clearly another spaceship within a few light-years away. Grant prepared the computer system to initiate communication with the foreign beings.

New Condition

Alexa, being the well-trained and organized leader, remained calm and began searching the database for information. There was clearly another spaceship within a few light-years away. Alexa prepared the computer system to initiate communication with the foreign beings.

Neither Condition

It was necessary to remain calm and begin searching the database for information. There was clearly another spaceship within a few light-years away. The next step was to prepare the computer system to initialize communication with the foreign beings. Once the computer was ready, the identity of the aliens could be established.

Experimental Probe Word: SPACESHIP [for before condition]; **KEYPAD** [for after condition]

Conclusion

Alexa turned on the monitor. Their hail was being answered. Hopefully, they would be cooperative. Often times they were, but there was no guarantee.

Filler Probe Word: LASER [for before condition]; **SPACESHIP** [for after condition]

Results

The same accuracy criteria were applied from the previous experiment: 45% of the participants were replaced because they did not satisfy the accuracy criteria. This high percentage of inadequate performances was most likely attributable to the fact that the object names in the narratives were mentioned only once in each narrative (in the first sentence of the first paragraph); in contrast, in Experiment 1 the character names were mentioned twice in the first paragraph (in the first and third sentence) and possibly rementioned in the second paragraph. Indeed, participants in Experiment 2 committed more errors, with the object names as probe words, than did participants in Experiment 1, with the character names as probe words, even at the baseline test point (i.e., 12% more errors at the *before* test point). In addition, participants' average verification latency in Experiment 2 was almost double that of Experiment 1 (575 ms vs. 918 ms at the *before* test point). In sum, Experiment 2 provided a harder task.

The design of the ANOVAs was the same as in the Experiment 1, and the results were similar, albeit attenuated slightly for the reasons just mentioned.

Verification latencies. A significant main effect was observed, $F1(3, 87) = 6.66, p < .001$, $F2(3, 31) = 4.43, p < .01$. As shown in Figure 3, the pattern was very

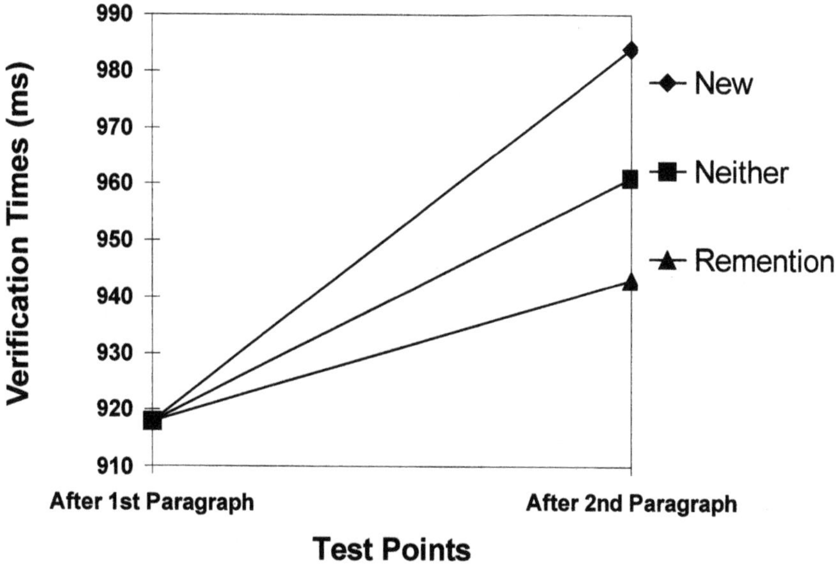

FIGURE 3 Participants' verification latencies (in ms) in Experiment 2.

similar to that of Experiment 1. In particular, we found that introducing a new character diminished the accessibility of the original character, even though the participants were tested on only an object closely associated with the main character and not the main character's actual name. Participants' verification latencies to an object associated with the main character were slower after reading a paragraph in which a new character was introduced ($M = 984$, $SE = 18$) than prior to reading a paragraph in which a new character was introduced ($M = 918$, $SE = 17$), $F(1, 87) = 18.571$, $p < .001$, $F2(1, 31) = 12.28$, $p < .001$. Participants' verification latencies to an object associated with the main character were also faster after reading a paragraph in which the main character was rementioned ($M = 943$, $SE = 17$) than after reading a paragraph in which a new character was introduced ($M = 984$, $SE = 18$), $F(1, 87) = 6.89$, $p < .001$, $F2(1, 31) = 3.72$, $p < .06$. As in Experiment 1, participants' verification latencies to the objects associated with the main character were statistically equivalent before reading a paragraph in which the main character was rementioned ($M = 918$, $SE = 17$) as after reading a paragraph in which the main character was rementioned ($M = 943$, $SE = 17$).

Verification errors. A significant main effect was observed when participants were considered a random effect, $F(3, 87) = 3.00$, $p < .05$, although not when probe words were considered a random effect, $F2(3, 31) = 2.18$, $p < .10$. Participants made more verification errors to an object associated with the main character after reading a paragraph in which a new character was introduced ($M = 18\%$, $SE =$

1%) than prior to reading a paragraph in which a new character was introduced (*M* = 13%, *SE* = 1%), $F(1, 87) = 4.74$, $p < .04$, $F2(1, 31) = 3.45$, $p < .06$.

Discussion

In Experiment 1, we observed that introducing a new character in a narrative produces a cost: An aforementioned character becomes less accessible. In Experiment 2, we observed that this reduction of accessibility is not specific to the main character's name, but can also be assayed by probing an object associated in the mental representation with the main character. Therefore, the results obtained in Experiment 2 allow us to rule out the possibility that results obtained in Experiment 1 were due to the remention of a specific character's name or to the introduction of a specific new character's name.

According to the Structure Building Framework, two mechanisms facilitate the cognitive processes of mapping and shifting, and hence the development of mental representations, during comprehension. The cognitive mechanism of enhancement increases the activation of related information; the cognitive mechanism of suppression decreases the activation of inappropriate or interfering information. Indeed, Gernsbacher (1997a) defined the cognitive mechanism of suppression as a mechanism that attenuates interference.

Gernsbacher (1997a) also reviewed numerous laboratory studies demonstrating the crucial role of suppression in attenuating the interference that often arises naturally during comprehension. These phenomena include lexical access, during which comprehenders often need to attenuate interfering lexical or phonological forms (Gernsbacher & Faust, 1991b; Gernsbacher, Robertson, & Werner, in press); anaphoric reference, during which comprehenders often need to attenuate other potential referents for anaphors such as pronouns (Gernsbacher, 1989, see also replications in English (MacDonald, & MacWhinney, 1990; Garnham Traxler, Oakhill, & Gernsbacher, 1996), Chinese (Sun, 1997), Korean (Lee, 1992), and American Sign Language (Emmorey, 1997); figurative language understanding, during which comprehenders often need to attenuate literal understandings (Gernsbacher, Keysar, Robertson, & Werner, in press; Gernsbacher & Robertson, 1999); and simultaneous interpretation, during which interpreters often need to attenuate interfering information such as cognates (Gernsbacher & Shlesinger, 1997).

Gernsbacher and others also reported that persons who are more skilled at comprehension (e.g., as assessed on a comprehension battery, such as the Nelson Denney) are more able to attenuate the interference that often arises during comprehension (De Beni, Palladino, Pazzaglia, & Cornoldi, 1998; Faust, Balota, Duchek, Gernsbacher, & Smith, 1997; Gernsbacher, 1997a, 1993, in press; Gernsbacher & Faust, 1991b; 1995; Gernsbacher, Varner, & Faust, 1990; Long, Seely, & Oppy, 1999; Palladino, Cornoldi, De Beni, & Pazzaglia, in press). In the final experiment that we report here, we explored whether more-skilled readers, who in previous research have been found to be more-skilled at suppression (i.e., attenuating interference), are also more skilled at attenuating the interference caused by introducing a new character into a narrative. Whereas previous research has investigated more- versus less-skilled comprehenders' ability to suppress interfering information at the lexical (Gernsbacher & Faust, 1991b) or sentence level, Experiment 3 investigated this distinction during narrative comprehension.

EXPERIMENT 3

The third experiment capitalized on the findings observed in our first two experiments, namely that introducing a new character into a narrative often leads to interference with (reduced accessibility of) a previously mentioned character. More- and less-skilled readers performed the experimental task of Experiment 1 so that we could examine whether more- and less-skilled readers differ in how well they can keep track of who is doing what to whom while reading a narrative.

Method

Participants. Ninety-six undergraduate students at the University of Wisconsin–Madison participated in the experiment to earn extra credit for an introductory psychology course.

Materials and Procedure. Participants completed a reading comprehension test, followed by the experimental task outlined in Experiment 1. The comprehension test (Gernsbacher & Varner, 1988) comprised four narratives, each one followed by 12 multiple-choice questions. Narratives and questions were presented on a computer screen. Of the participants, 48 were classified as more-skilled readers (one third), and 48 were classified as less-skilled readers on the basis of their performance on the reading comprehension test (one third). The 48 more-skilled readers scored higher than 79% on the comprehension test, whereas less-skilled readers scored lower than 67%. Selection criteria were fixed at 50% for verification accuracy and greater than 250 ms for verification latency: 5% of skilled and less-skilled readers were eliminated because they did not satisfy the criteria.

Following the completion of the reading comprehension test, subsequent materials and procedures were identical to those outlined in Experiment 1.

Results

Analyses of the data were again conducted separately for verification errors and verification latency. Reading skill was included as a between- variable.

Verification latencies. A significant main effect was observed for test point, $F(3, 94) = 80.81, p < .001$. As in Experiment 1, participants' verification latencies to the main character's name were faster after reading a second paragraph in which the main character was rementioned ($M = 514$, $SE = 19$) than after reading a second paragraph in which neither the main character was rementioned nor a new character was introduced ($M = 621$, $SE = 23$), $F1(1, 95) = 76.00, p < .001$. Comparing the data from these two conditions (verification latencies in the remention condition and verification latencies in the neither condition) allows us to gauge that participants reaped a statistically significant benefit: Rementioning the main character increased its accessibility.

In addition, as in Experiment 1, participants in Experiment 3 reaped a statistically significant cost, when indexed by their verification latencies. Participants' verification latencies to the main character's name were slower after reading a second paragraph in which a new character was introduced ($M = 704$, $SE = 28$) than after reading a second paragraph in which neither the main character was rementioned nor a new character was introduced ($M = 621$, $SE = 23$), $F1(1, 95) = 29.41, p < .001$. Participants' verification latencies to the main character's name were statistically equivalent before reading a second paragraph in which the main character was rementioned ($M = 523$, $SE = 19$) as after reading a second paragraph in which the main character was rementioned ($M = 514$, $SE = 19$).

Using verification latencies as a dependent variable, we also observed a significant main effect for reading skill, $F(1, 94) = 10.73, p < .01$: More-skilled readers' verification latencies($M = 524$, $SE = 14$) were an average 132 ms faster than less-skilled readers' verification latencies ($M = 656$, $SE = 19$). However, there were no interactions with reading skill observed when considering the verification latencies as dependent variable.

Verification errors. A significant main effect was observed for test point, $F(3, 94) = 19.82$, $p < .001$, but no main effect was observed for reading skill. Rather, we observed a significant interaction between reading skill and test point, $F(3, 94) = 4.18, p < .01$. As shown in Figure 4, less-skilled readers (indicated by the solid lines) showed a statistically significant cost: Less-skilled readers made 9% more errors when verifying the main character's name after reading a paragraph in which a new character was introduced ($M = 16\%$, $SE = 2.1\%$) than after reading a paragraph in which neither a new character was introduced nor the main character was rementioned ($M = 7\%$, $SE = 1.6\%$), $F(1, 47) = 17.80, p < .001$. In contrast, as shown in Figure 4, more-skilled readers (as indicated by the dashed

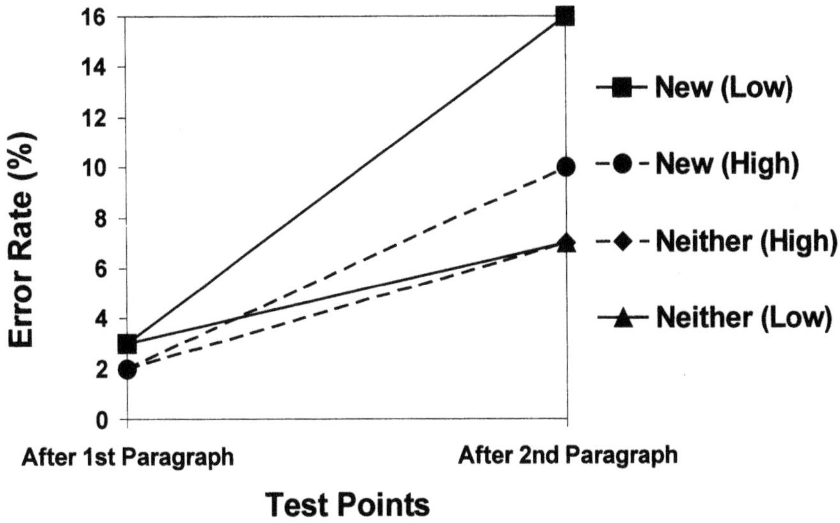

FIGURE 4 Participants' verification error rate (in percentage) in Experiment 3. "Low" refers to the less-skilled readers and "high" refers to the more-skilled readers.

line) did not show a statistically significant cost: More-skilled readers did not make statistically more errors when verifying the main character's name after reading a paragraph in which a new character was introduced ($M = 9.9\%$, $SE = 1.7\%$) than after reading a paragraph in which neither a new character was introduced nor the main character was rementioned ($M = 7\%$, $SE = 1.4\%$), $F(1, 47) \sim 2.0$.

Discussion

Experiment 3 demonstrated that less-skilled readers showed high cost, in their accuracy, when a new character was introduced. In contrast, more-skilled readers seemed to be little affected, in terms of their accuracy, when a new character was introduced. If introducing a new character causes interference, as we have suggested, these data support the hypothesis that more-skilled readers are more skilled at attenuating interference (i.e., suppression).

CONCLUSIONS

The experiments reported here suggest that successful narrative comprehension involves taking advantage of rementioned information and reducing the costs associated with interfering information. In each experiment, participants read narratives in which a main character was introduced. In a subsequent section of the narrative, the main character was either rementioned, a new character was introduced, or no character was mentioned (anaphorically or otherwise). Results from all three experiments provide evidence that mental access to the main character is strengthened when that character is rementioned, and interfered with when a new character is introduced. When asked to verify whether they had seen the main character's name in a narrative, readers were consistently faster and more accurate to say that they had when the main character's name had been rementioned. In contrast, readers were consistently slower and less accurate to verify that they had seen the main character's name when the narrative introduced a new character. We were able to unambiguously interpret these results as benefits and costs because (unlike previous experiments) we included a neutral 'condition.' We also were able to investigate whether the effect we observed was specific to our probe words being names by testing the accessibility of an object associated with the main character. As with the main character, per se, we found that an object associated with the main character increased in accessibility when that main character was rementioned and decreased in accessibility when a new character was introduced. Lastly, we explored whether reading skill affected the ability to attenuate the interference caused by the introduction of a new character. We found that more-skilled readers, who have previously been shown to be more skilled at attenuating interference during comprehension (i.e., suppression) did not show in their verification accuracy a cost when a new character was introduced.

These data were consistent with studies on the mental representation created when reading individual sentences (Gernsbacher, 1989) and extend these findings to the level of the narrative. Moreover, these data were consistent with the tenets of the Structure Building Framework, which assumes that once readers have laid a foundation based on the most relevant textual information (in this case, the main character of each narrative), subsequent information is either perceived as relevant or irrelevant; if relevant, the information is mapped onto the existing information; if less relevant comprehenders shift to build a new substructure. In Experiment 1, readers were significantly faster and more accurate to identify the main character (e.g., *Grant*) when he or she was rementioned than when a new character (e.g., *Alexa*) was introduced. According to the Structure Building Framework, readers would have constructed a mental representation of the narrative based on the main character; the introduction of a new character poses as an interference to this representation, thus, the increase in verification latencies that we see in the present experiments when a new character is introduced. Conversely, by rementioning the main character, it becomes enhanced in the reader's mental representation, accounting for the faster verification latencies when the main character was rementioned. As shown in Experiment 2, these findings persisted even when the probe word was an object associated with that character rather than the name of the actual character. This is also consistent with the Structure Building Framework, as it assumes that an object associated with the main character would be mapped onto the mental representation founded on the main character. The data collected with more and less-skilled comprehenders in Experiment 3 is equally consistent with the Structure Building Framework: More-skilled comprehenders are characterized by more efficient suppression.

The experiments reported here illustrate that readers must keep track of who is doing what to whom to successfully read and comprehend a narrative. This narrative tracking results in a mental representation that is built on the most relevant textual information, with subsequent information being either relevant or irrelevant to the preexisting foundation. Skilled readers are therefore able to filter through narrative details with relatively little exertion by capitalizing on the benefits gained from relevant information, and minimizing the costs incurred by less-relevant information.

ACKNOWLEDGMENTS

This research was supported by grants awarded to Morton Ann Gernsbacher from the National Institutes of Health (R01-NS-29926) and the Army Research Institute (DASW0194-K-004). Portions of these data were presented at the 68th annual meeting of the Midwestern Psychological Association (May 2–4, 1996; Chicago, IL).

REFERENCES

De Beni, R., Palladino, P., Pazzaglia, F., & Cornoldi, C. (1998). Increases in intrusion errors and working memory deficit of poor comprehenders. *Quarterly Journal of Experimental Psychology: Human Experimental Psychology, 51A*, 305–320.

Dell, G. S., McKoon, G., & Ratcliff, R. (1983). The activation of antecedent information during the processing of anaphoric reference in reading. *Journal of Verbal Learning and Verbal Behavior, 22*, 121–132.

Emmorey, K. (1997). Non-antecedent suppression in American Sign Language. *Language and Cognitive Processes, 12*, 103–119.

Faust, M. E., Balota, D. A., Duchek, J. A., Gernsbacher, M. G., & Smith, S. D. (1997). Inhibitory control during sentence processing in individuals with dementia of the Alzheimer type. *Brain and Language, 57*, 225–253.

Garnham, A., Traxler, M. J., Oakhill, J. V., & Gernsbacher, M. G. (1996). The locus of implicit causality effects in comprehension. *Journal of Memory and Language, 35*, 517–543.

Gernsbacher, M. A. (1989). Mechanisms that improve referential access. *Cognition, 32*, 99–156.

Gernsbacher, M. A. (1990). *Language comprehension as structure building*. Hillsdale, NJ: Lawrence Erlbaum Associates, Inc.

Gernsbacher, M. A. (1991). Cognitive processes and mechanisms in language comprehension: The structure building framework. In G. H. Bower (Ed.), *The psychology of learning and motivation* (pp. 217–263). New York: Academic.

Gernsbacher, M. A. (1993). Less skilled readers have less efficient suppression mechanisms. *Psychological Science, 4*, 294–298.
Gernsbacher, M. A. (1995). The Structure Building Framework: What it is, what it might also be, and why. In B. K. Britton & A. C. Graesser (Eds.), *Models of text understanding* (pp. 289–311). Hillsdale, NJ: Lawrence Erlbaum Associates, Inc.
Gernsbacher, M. A. (1997a). Attenuating interference during comprehension: The role of suppression. In D. L. Medin (Ed.), *The psychology of learning and motivation* (pp. 85–104). San Diego, CA: Academic.
Gernsbacher, M. A. (1997b). Two decades of structure building. *Discourse Processes, 23*, 265–304.
Gernsbacher, M. A., & Faust, M. (1991a). The mechanism of suppression: A component of general comprehension skill. *Journal of Experimental Psychology: Learning, Memory and Cognition, 17*, 245–262.
Gernsbacher, M. A., & Faust, M. (1991b). The role of suppression in sentence comprehension. In G. B. Simpson (Ed.), *Understanding word and sentence* (pp. 97–128). Amsterdam: North Holland.
Gernsbacher, M. A., & Faust, M. (1995). Skilled suppression. In F. N. Dempster & C. N. Brainerd's (Eds.), *Interference and inhibition in cognition* (pp. 295–327). San Diego, CA: Academic.
Gernsbacher, M. A., Keysar, B., Robertson, R. R. W., & Werner, N. K. (in press). The role of suppression and enhancement in understanding metaphors. *Journal of Memory and Language, 45*, 433–450.
Gernsbacher, M. A., & Robertson, R. R. W. (1999). The role of suppression in figurative language comprehension. *Journal of Pragmatics, 31*, 1619–1630.
Gernsbacher, M. A., Robertson, R. R. W., & Werner, N. K. (2000). The costs and benefits of meaning. In D. S. Gorfein (Ed.), *On the consequences of meaning selection* (pp. 119– 137). Washington, DC: American Psychological Association.
Gernsbacher, M. A., & Shlesinger, M. (1997). The proposed role of suppression in simultaneous interpretation. *Interpreting, 2*, 119–140.
Gernsbacher, M. A., & Varner, K. R. (1988). *The multi-media comprehension battery* (Tech. Rep. No. 88-03). Eugene: University of Oregon, Institute of Cognitive and Decision Sciences.
Gernsbacher, M. A., Varner, K. R., & Faust, M. (1990). Investigating differences in general comprehension skill. *Journal of Experimental Psychology: Learning, Memory, and Cognition, 16*, 430–445.
Gordon, P. C., Hendrick, R., & Foster, K. L. (2000). Language comprehension and probe-list memory. *Journal of Experimental Psychology: Learning, Memory, and Cognition, 26*, 766–775.
Lee, J. (1992). On-line processing of pronoun resolution in reading. Unpublished doctoral dissertation, Korea University, Seoul, Korea.
Long, D. L., & de Ley, L. (2000). Understanding anaphors in story dialogue. *Memory & Cognition, 28*, 731–738.
Long, D. L., Seely, M. R., & Oppy, B. J. (1999). The strategic nature of less skilled readers' suppression problems. *Discourse Processes, 27*, 281–302.
MacDonald, M. C., & MacWhinney, B. (1990). Measuring inhibition and facilitation effects from pronouns. *Journal of Memory and Language, 29*, 469–492.
Nordlie, J., Dopkins, S., & Johnson, M. (2001). Words in a sentence become less accessible when an anaphor is resolved. *Memory & Cognition, 29*, 355–362.
Palladino, P., Cornoldi, C., De Beni, R., & Pazzaglia, F. (2001). Working memory and updating processes in reading comprehension. *Memory & Cognition, 29*, 344 –354.
Sun, Y. (1997). The immediacy effects in pronoun resolution in Chinese comprehension. Unpublished doctoral dissertation, Beijing Normal University, Beijing, China.

DISCOURSE PROCESSES, *37*(2), 165–186

Fluctuations in the Availability of Information During Reading: Capturing Cognitive Processes Using the Landscape Model

Tracy Linderholm
Department of Educational Psychology
University of Florida

Sandra Virtue
Department of Psychology
Northwestern University

Yuhtsuen Tzeng
Center for Teachers' Education
National Chung Cheng University

Paul van den Broek
Department of Educational Psychology
University of Minnesota

In this investigation, we examine the availability of text elements over the course of reading a text. We describe the Landscape model (van den Broek, Young, Tzeng, & Linderholm, 1999) that captures, in one theoretical framework, multiple cognitive processes during reading and the resulting fluctuating activations of text elements. To demonstrate the applicability of the Landscape model, we simulate the availability of text elements in two reading situations. First, the Landscape model is shown to incorporate readers' specific purpose for reading, affecting the availability of text elements as a function of different standards of coherence. Second, the Landscape model is

Correspondence and requests for reprints should be sent to Paul van den Broek, Department of Educational Psychology, University of Minnesota, Burton Hall, 178 Pillsbury Drive S.E., Minneapolis, MN 55455. E-mail: pvdbroek@umn.edu shown to incorporate readers' background knowledge during reading, allowing readers to detect inconsistencies in a text. Theoretical accounts such as the Landscape model extend our understanding of—and to investigate—the process of reading by providing information about the availability of text elements in a unified theoretical framework, thereby extending and complementing behavioral data.

As a reader proceeds through a text, information continuously changes in its activation in the reader's mind. One important, and obvious, reason is that with each new text segment new information is introduced and activated. Yet, there are other potential reasons as well. For example, the activation of new information may come at the expense of the information that was activated before the new text segment was read. Also, it is possible that the newly activated information itself triggers activation of further information by means of various automatic or strategic processes or both. Whatever factors are involved, the resulting fluctuations affect the availability of information to the reader at each point during reading and, hence, are bound to have a profound impact on the reader's readiness for and ability to process the text (e.g., Gernsbacher, 1997; Gerrig & McKoon, 1998; van den Broek et al., 1999).

If we want to understand the processes involved in reading comprehension, it is essential to understand the factors that influence the fluctuations in activation. From a practical point of view, understanding the process, and where it may fail, leads to an understanding of why readers struggle, and suggests where to focus attempts for intervention and remediation. In this article, we provide a theoretical and computational framework for capturing the fluctuating activations during reading and the factors that affect these fluctuations. The framework, the Landscape model, integrates theoretical notions that have been corroborated in past research as well as new insights into one comprehensive model (a Windows-based copy of the computational simulation is available from the third author). A major benefit of using a computational model to study phenomena important in reading, such as the on-line activation of elements, is that we can investigate several processes of reading simultaneously, which is difficult in exclusively behavioral studies. Another benefit is that the model can be used as a methodological tool, to contrast and test hypotheses, to generate predictions, to contrast different types of readers and reading situations, and so on. In this article, we review the theoretical framework of the Landscape model, its architecture, and empirical evidence for the validity of the model (van den Broek, Risden, Fletcher & Thurlow, 1996; van den Broek et al., 1999). In addition, we show how the model can simulate the availability of information on-line in two novel reading situations.

SOURCES OF FLUCTUATIONS IN ACTIVATION

The theoretical framework for the Landscape model assumes that concepts fluctuate in their activation along a continuum during reading rather than in an all-or-none manner (see Gerrig & McKoon, 1998). Furthermore, concepts are activated in a cyclical manner, one input segment at a time. In this article, we use individual sentences as the input segments (Kintsch & van Dijk, 1978; Trabasso, Secco, van den Broek, 1984), but a different definition of 'input segment' can be chosen depending on one's theoretical perspective. Several potential sources of activation are implemented in the model's architecture. First, the current text provides new input to the reader and, in doing so, induces the reader to activate new information. Second, information that was activated in the prior reading cycle is readily available and therefore may be carried over, in whole or in part. Third, a reader may *reinstate* information that was activated in a previous reading cycle, that is, it was explicitly mentioned in the text or it was activated from any of the other sources at this earlier cycle. Fourth, a reader may activate *background knowledge.* Together, these sources determine the patterns of activations—the *activation vector*—at each point during reading. The first of the potential sources of activation, the current text, is self-evident. Indeed, if in a specific instance a text does not affect—implicitly or explicitly—the activation in a 'reader' then the person is not actually reading. The second source, carry-over from the prior reading cycle, likewise needs little elaboration. Although models of text comprehension differ in the details of mechanism for such carry over, they all posit that some residue of the activations in one processing cycle lingers into the next (e.g., Fletcher & Bloom, 1988; Kintsch, 1988; McKoon & Ratcliff, 1992).

The third and fourth sources, reinstatement from prior reading cycles and activation of background knowledge, need some elaboration. In a reinstatement, information that has been processed in a prior cycle, and since has decayed in activation, is reactivated. Reinstated information may include the actual textual information from the prior cycle but also other information, such as inferences and associations to background knowledge that had been activated during that cycle. Activation of background knowledge involves access to and retrieval from semantic memory.

Two types of mechanisms are involved in reinstatements and background knowledge activations, according to the theoretical framework in the Landscape model. The first type of mechanism is *cohort activation.* Cohort activation consists of a spread of activation from the currently activated information to its associates, that is, its *cohort,* in the episodic memory representation that has been formed over the course of the preceding cycles (resulting in reinstatement) or the reader's semantic memory representation (resulting in activation of background knowledge). Each element in a concept's cohort is activated to the degree that it is associated with the primary concept, and the concepts that make up the cohort change throughout the reading process (see the following discussion of the evolving episodic representation). *Cohort activation* is memory-based, and is fast and passive. This mechanism is similar to those described in other models of reading (e.g., the resonance model, Myers & O'Brien, 1998). The theoretical assumptions of the Landscape model presume that the process of cohort activation is identical for both episodic and semantic memory. Indeed, recent evidence validates this assumption (Rizzella & O'Brien, 2002).

The second type of mechanism for reinstating information and for activating background knowledge is *coherence-based retrieval.* Coherence-based retrieval is the strategic and deliberate retrieval of information in an attempt to understand the current text and, thereby, create coherence. In the case of reinstatements, coherence-based retrieval may take the form of access to the episodic memory representation that has been developed over the prior cycles or of other actions, such as actual look-backs through the text (Goldman & Saul, 1990). In the case of retrieving background knowledge, it involves a search of the reader's knowledge base. Coherence-based retrieval usually is slow and effortful (e.g., Bloom, Fletcher, van den Broek, Reitz, & Shapiro, 1990). Thus, the model incorporates both bottom-up (cohort activation) and top-down processes (coherence-based retrieval).

According to the theoretical framework of the model, the four potential sources together determine the patterns of activation that take place during reading. The degree to which each source contributes varies across readers and situations. A central role in determining the involvement of each source is played by the reader's *standards of coherence* (van den Broek, Risden, & Husebye-Hartmann, 1995). These standards reflect the degree of comprehension that a reader attempts to attain during the reading of a text. Several factors may influence the specific standard that a reader has. For example, the reader's purpose for reading the text is bound to affect the choice of standards (Linderholm & van den Broek, 2002; van den Broek, Lorch, Linderholm, & Gustafson, 2001). Likewise, background knowledge, difficulty of the text, the presence of distractions, reader fatigue, comprehension strategies, and so on, may determine the standards (Graesser, Singer, & Trabasso, 1994; van den Broek et al., 1995). The standards of coherence play a particularly important role in prompting inference generation involving coherence-based retrievals: When a reader perceives a breakdown in the coherence reflected in his/her standards, he or she is likely to engage in strategic processes to remedy the breakdown by generating reinstatements and inferences based on background knowledge. Thus, the standards of coherence a reader employs influence the sources of activations that are accessed. This, in turn, affects what elements are activated during reading.

The architecture of the Landscape model is able to simulate a specific standard of coherence for the reader. For example, there are different kinds of coherence that a reader can pursue, including referential, causal, spatial, temporal coherence (cf. the Event-Indexing model of reading; Zwaan, Langston, & Graesser, 1995). Of these, referential and causal coherence have been found to play a particularly important role in comprehension. Prior Landscape model simulations compared different input parameters, which corresponded to different standards of coherence, to human recall data. The results showed that when the model is allowed to process *both* referential and causal relations, the simulation output is highly correlated to actual human recall ($r = .69$). Moreover, the Landscape model simulation output is correlated with recall to a much greater extent compared to when the model is allowed to process *only* referential or *only* causal relations (van den Broek, 2002). Accordingly, the implementation of the Landscape model in the remainder of this article includes referential and causal coherence as two components of the average readers' standards of coherence.

In summary, according to the theoretical framework of the Landscape model, during reading, concepts fluctuate in their activations as a function of the text segment that is being read, carry-over from the preceding cycle, as well as of automatic and strategic processes that (re)activate information from the episodic memory representation of the text and from background knowledge. In the architectural design of the Landscape model, the reader's standards of coherence play an important role in determining the contributions of the various sources, in particular of those that involve strategic processes (e.g., to resolve coherence breaks).

THE EPISODIC MEMORY REPRESENTATION

Although the focus of this article is on how the Landscape model captures the activation of concepts during reading, the model also captures the developing memory representation. This evolving representation provides the basis for cohort activation and, thus, affects what currently is activated by the reader. Therefore, we briefly describe how the episodic memory of a text is formed in the Landscape model.

In current theories of reading, the episodic memory representation of a text is conceived of as a network of interconnected nodes: The nodes represent the individual concepts that are encountered or activated during reading, and the connections represent the semantic relations that are established between the concepts (e.g., Goldman & Varma, 1995; Langston & Trabasso, 1999). Nodes and connections in a network differ in their memory strengths. In the architectural design of the Landscape model, the activation vectors representing the concepts that are activated at each reading cycle help create the gradually emerging network representation of a text over the course of reading. With each new cycle, new nodes and connections are added to the representation and ones already present in the network change in strength. The *amount of change* in the representation is a function of the new activation vector: the stronger a node is activated, the greater the change in its representation, and the stronger two concepts are coactivated the greater the change in connection between the two concepts in the memory representation. However, the change is asymptotic because it also depends on the representational strength of the node or connection prior to the current cycle: The stronger a concept or relation between concepts is represented, the smaller the impact of additional co-activations. The node and connection strength of the evolving network influence subsequent activation vectors, for example, by providing the basis for cohort activation. Thus, the Landscape model consists of a dynamic and reciprocal relation that exists between the changing activation vectors and the emerging episodic memory representation of the text.

To summarize, the architecture of the Landscape model consists of activation vectors that lead to a gradually emerging episodic memory representation of the text during reading. In turn, this episodic memory representation partly determines the activation vectors in the model. Through cohort activation a currently activated concept will reactivate related information in the episodic memory representation. The more strongly the earlier information is encoded or connected to a concept in the current reading cycle, the more available it is for reactivation in the current cycle.

COMPUTATIONAL SIMULATION OF THE FLUCTUATING ACTIVATIONS OF ELEMENTS DURING READING

Central to the theoretical framework in the Landscape model is the notion that reading is a dynamic process in which many factors combine to create fluctuating activation vectors, eventually resulting in a stable memory representation of a text. To consider the combined effect of all these factors on the constantly changing patterns of accessibility of information over the course of reading an entire text, the factors are implemented in a computational simulation of the reading process.

The architecture of the computational implementation of the Landscape model includes activation from each of the four sources outlined previously. Cohort activation takes place according to a spread of activation parameter similar to what is described in resonance models (Myers & O'Brien, 1998) and varies between the values of 0, indicating no cohort activation, and 1, indicating a high degree of cohort activation. Moreover, concepts activated in one cycle are carried over but, because they compete with concepts activated as part of a new cycle, they will gradually decay. The 'default' standard of coherence includes referential and causal coherence, reflecting the prominence of these standards in current models of reading comprehension. These standards dictate the coherence-based retrieval processes. Concepts that are explicitly mentioned receive the highest activation (5 on the 5-point scale used for the illustrations in this article). Concepts activated as a result of a reader's causal and referential standards of coherence (i.e., reinstated or retrieved from background knowledge) receive slightly less activation (4 on the 5-point scale), concepts activated to establish enabling relations even less (3), and concepts with associative relations the least (2). The resulting activation vectors gradually create a memory representation of the concepts. Each activation of a particular concept strengthens its memory trace. Likewise, each coactivation of concepts results in a change in their connection strength, as a function of the cross-product of activations for the two concepts. The resulting learning curve follows an asymptotic delta rule, which is sensitive to the degree of 'newness' of the currently encountered concept and results in an asymmetrical connection between concepts at retrieval. This is important because some concepts may be more predictive (or strongly associated) to concepts in one direction (e.g., 'bread' is more predictive of 'butter' than 'butter' is of 'bread'). To summarize, the computational simulation allows one to capture a range of cognitive processes essential to comprehension and memory for texts.

EMPIRICAL SUPPORT FOR THE LANDSCAPE MODEL

The theoretical framework of the Landscape model, and its computational architecture, has received empirical support from comparisons between simulations of the reading process and human data (for details, see van den Broek, Risden, Fletcher, & Thurlow, 1996). Human participants read simple narrative stories and rated (on a 5-point Likert-type scale) how strongly they thought that each concept in each sentence of the story was activated during reading. Participants' ratings were averaged, thus providing a human 'landscape' of activation vectors for concepts. The human landscape was compared to a Landscape model simulation of the story, with causal and referential relations as standards of coherence. The correlation between the activation values in the empirical and theoretical landscapes was very high ($r = .73, p < .01$). Thus, the Landscape model is able to capture the activation of concepts during reading as reported by actual readers.

The second part of this validation study involved a comparison of the Landscape model's final text representation to human recall. The Landscape model's predictions of human participants' recall, based on the node and connection strengths calculated in the simulation, were highly correlated to the observed frequency of recall by human readers ($r = .70, p < .01$). In addition to frequency of recall, the Landscape model also accurately predicted the actual order in which the readers recalled the concepts, with stronger nodes being recalled first, followed by those with strong connections to the initial nodes. Thus, the Landscape model has been shown to have empirical validity, with the predicted online activations matching those of humans and off-line retrieval values capturing human recall.

EXTENDING THE LANDSCAPE MODEL TO MORE COMPLEX READING SITUATIONS

To demonstrate the usefulness of the Landscape model for capturing the availability of elements in more complex reading circumstances, we next illustrate how the model simulates activation in two such situations. In the first simulation, the Landscape model is used to capture how the reading process is adjusted to fit reading purpose—and corresponding standards of coherence—of the reader. In the second simulation, the Landscape model is used to capture the detection of inconsistencies.

The Influence of Reading Purpose on Availability during Reading

Recent behavioral evidence supports the idea that a reader's purpose can alter the elements that are available during reading. For example, college students self-report that they engage in different kinds of reading processes when reading for study versus entertainment (Lorch, Lorch, & Klusewitz, 1993). In addition, verbal protocol results show that readers alter their cognitive processes to fit their purposes for reading (Linderholm & van den Broek, 2002; Narvaez, van den Broek, & Ruiz, 1999). In terms of specific cognitive processes, when readers are reading to study they engage in more processes aimed at creating coherence than when they are reading for entertainment (van den Broek et al., 2001). For example, readers produce more backward inferences, predictive inferences, and paraphrases when reading to study, whereas they produce more associations and editorial remarks when reading for entertainment.

Although behavioral studies demonstrate that the availability of different text elements depends on the reader's purpose for reading, we do not know how the various cognitive processes and properties of the reading process (e.g., sources of activation, cohort activation, properties of the memory representation) contribute to reading purpose effects on the availability of text elements. The Landscape model simulation posits that different reading purposes—and the corresponding standards of coherence—lead to different inferential processes, thereby producing different patterns of availability. We illustrate this in the context of expository text reading. By showing the model's applicability to expository texts, we extend the model in yet another way, as previous simulations have focused on narrative texts.

The expository text used in this simulation was adapted from an article published in *Scientific American* entitled, "Why American Songbirds are Vanishing." (van den Broek et al., 2001; see Appendix A). This text is 32 sentences in length, contains approximately 800 words, and was selected for its informational and interest value. The text describes a problem in nature, the decline of songbirds, and several hypotheses on its potential cause. Each of the 32 sentences of the text constituted a single input cycle in the simulation.

The relation(s) that each sentence has to other sentences was analyzed to determine which relations would be processed under each of two reading purposes, for study and for entertainment. Because the text is expository in nature, we added two types of relations, logical and contrastive, to the referential and causal relations already described for narratives (see van den Broek et al., 1999; van den Broek, Virtue, Everson, Tzeng, & Sung, 2002). Logical relations are ideas that follow by implication from an antecedent (e.g., ideas that can be connected through terms such as herefore whereas contrast relations compare two ideas (e.g., ideas that can be connected through ut or n contrast . Two independent raters agreed on the referential, causal, logical, and contrastive relations present between sentences.

In line with the architecture of the Landscape model previously described, concepts necessary for referential, causal, and logical connections received activation values of 4. In addition, concepts involved in contrastive relations received an activation value of 3, under the assumption that the average reader expands mental effort on these relations ut less so than on other relations. The input parameters of the two reading purposes were based on the theoretical assumptions of the model; readers in a study purpose condition are expected to execute more complex processes (explicit, referential, causal, logical, and contrastive relations), to achieve a higher standard of coherence. In contrast, readers in an entertainment purpose condition should execute less complex processes (explicit, referential relations) for a more relaxed standard of coherence.

For each reading purpose condition, the obtained activation values for main ideas were summed across reading cycles. The outcome of the simulation showed that the sums of activation across the two reading purpose conditions differed. Specifically, a hypothetical reader reading for study keeps sentence information more highly activated across cycles than a hypothetical reader reading for entertainment, $t(62) = 2.59$, $SE = 1.29$, $p = .006$. This finding suggests that, in the computational simulation, executing more complex cognitive processes and having a strict standard of coherence—such as when reading for study—results in the activation of more elements throughout reading.

To illustrate how the model allows one to inspect differences in the specific activation patterns between the study and entertainment purpose simulations, we consider the availability of one of the main ideas, what is not so obvious is why forest-dwelling migratory songbirds are also vanishing (Sentence 2). This idea is highly causally connected to other main ideas and motivates much of the remainder of the text. Several hypotheses are presented later in the text to explain why songbirds were on the decline. Differences in activation for the ideas in Sentence 2 between reading purposes are expected because readers in this study purpose condition (compared to readers in the entertainment purpose condition) would generate causal connections between each of the hypotheses presented at various points in the text and the original problem posed in Sentence 2. Thus, the ideas in Sentence 2 will not be as highly activated across cycles because they are not often directly referenced in the text.

The Landscape model simulation shows more activation of Sentence 2 ideas across reading cycles in the study purpose simulation compared to in the entertainment purpose simulation, $t\,(62) = 2.6$, $SE = .40$, $p = .004$ (see Figure 1). Thus, reading for a study purpose resulted in more backward inferences and in a higher activation of the ideas represented in Sentence 2. In addition, this simulation shows

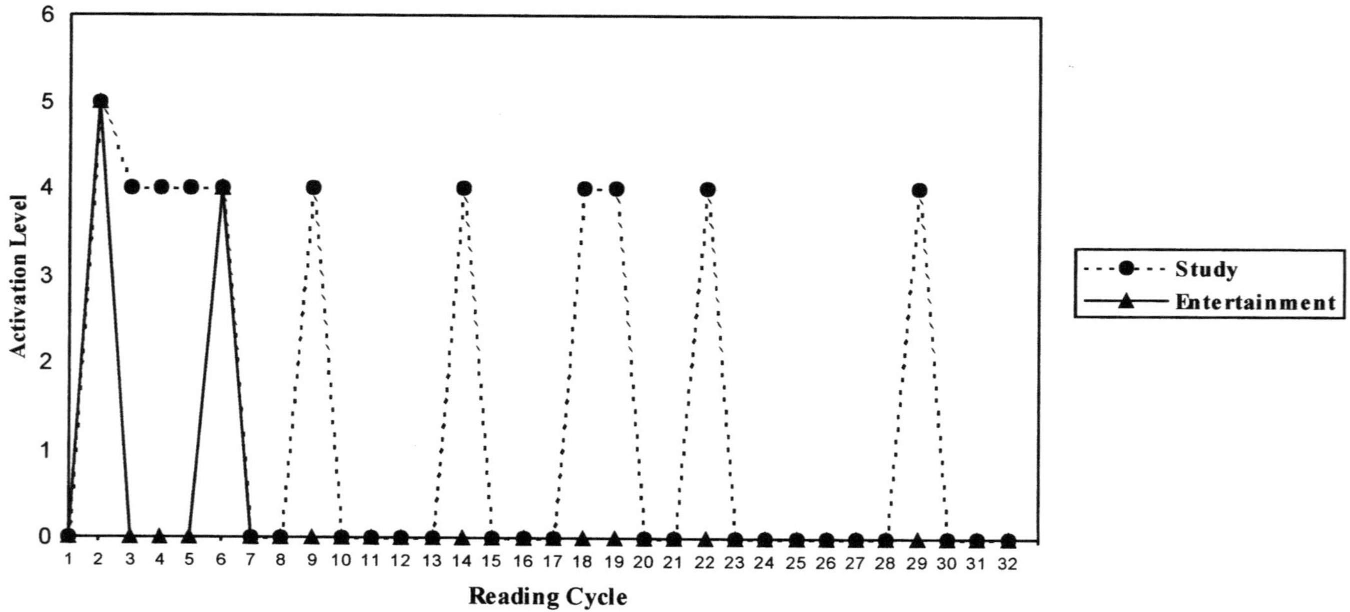

FIGURE 1 The Landscape model's simulated activation patterns of the idea presented in Sentence 2 (e.g., Why are songbirds vanishing?) as a function of reading purpose.

that Sentence 2 ideas were not highly activated throughout reading when the hypothetical reader only processes referential and the most obvious causal relations, as in an entertainment purpose reading condition.

The Landscape model simulation results were compared to behavioral results (Linderholm & van den Broek, 2002). In the behavioral study, readers were asked to read the songbirds passage for either study or entertainment purposes and perform a think-aloud task as they did so. Verbal responses were coded into several cognitive processing categories including causal connections (i.e., backward inferences). The behavioral results show that readers in this study condition made more causal connections than did readers in the entertainment condition, $t(2120) = -1.68$, $SE = .02$, $p = .045$. These quantitative, behavioral results are consistent with the results obtained in the Landscape model simulation. Certainly, qualitative differences between reading purpose conditions exist as well and could be simulated in the future.

Most important, the Landscape model simulation shows that activation patterns for reading elements related to different reading purposes vary substantially. If a reading purpose (e.g., reading for study) requires more in-depth processing of certain types of relations, relevant elements receive high activation values. In psychological terms, readers must expend more cognitive energy on more complex cognitive processes when their standard of coherence is high, resulting in higher activation of the elements involved in those processes. In addition, as a result of receiving higher activation values, these elements become more strongly associated with other elements that also are important for understanding the text. Thus, the higher standard will result in a stronger and richer network representation of the text in memory.

In summary, the Landscape model captures the fluctuation of text elements during the reading process as a function of different standards of coherence and can be extended to the modeling of expository text. Thus, the Landscape model can be used to examine the availability of different text elements, in expository or narrative texts, and explain what readers comprehend and how they go about tracking ideas when they have varying reading purposes.

The Detection of Inconsistencies during Reading

The availability of concepts in readers' episodic memory representations plays an important role in many theories of text comprehension (e.g., Kintsch, 1988; van Dijk & Kintsch, 1983). Episodic memory representation refers to the reader's developing mental representation of information contained in the text itself together with whatever information was retrieved from his or her general, semantic background knowledge to understand that prior text (Trabasso & Suh, 1993). In the Landscape model, information from this episodic memory representation is reactivated in later reading cycles via both strategic and automatic processes. The strategic processes result from the reader's attempt to maintain coherence, to map new information onto information from the proceeding text that is no longer in working memory. The automatic processes consist of cohort activation, by which activation spreads from the concepts in the current reading cycle to the episodic memory representation. The availability of the episodic memory representation helps readers establish and maintain coherence during reading.

In addition to allowing readers to establish coherence, the reactivation of information from prior cycles may lead readers to detect inconsistencies within a text. The Landscape model easily captures the processes by which readers detect inconsistencies. As previously described, in the Landscape model information from prior reading cycles can be reactivated through cohort activation. According to cohort activation, concepts in the current cycle reactivate concepts in the episodic memory representation of the text and–through spread of activation–of other concepts that have become connected in the episodic network with the initial set of reactivated concepts. If reactivated information co-occurs or is coactivated with information in the current cycle that is inconsistent, the foundation is laid for a detection of the inconsistency. Furthermore, because concepts can differ in their representational strengths, and in the strengths of their connections to other concepts, the extent of reactivation of a concept varies when an inconsistency is encountered.

To demonstrate how cohort activation helps readers to reactivate their episodic memory representation to detect an inconsistency, a simulation was performed on a text taken from Rizzella and O'Brien (1996). The text describes an old man taking a walk in his neighborhood. The text is considered 'inconsistent' because it first describes the man as old and weak but later describes him as strong enough to quickly run and pick up an injured boy in the street (see Appendix B). The episodic memory representation of the text is labeled as 'old' and the inconsistent portion of the later text is labeled as 'young' in the simulation. For the Landscape model simulation, the text was parsed into major concepts across 20 sentences with 56 concepts. Each sentence represented 1 reading cycle in the model, creating 20 reading cycles. Two experimenters agreed on causal, referential, and enabling relations throughout the texts.

To examine how the availability of concepts from a reader's episodic memory representation of the text highlights text inconsistencies via cohort activation, consider the Landscape model's activation of the set summarized by "old" and "young" at cycle 6 versus cycle 17 in Figure 2. Because the reader has an episodic memory representation of the story character, Bill, as being old, weak, needing a cane to walk, and so on, the memory trace of this aspect of the character is strong because it is now interconnected with other aspects of the text. At cycle 17, where the text describes the man as able to run quickly to help a hurt boy, cohort activation allows the inconsistency to be noticed. Suddenly learning that the man can run quickly reactivates the part of the episodic memory representation that pertains to

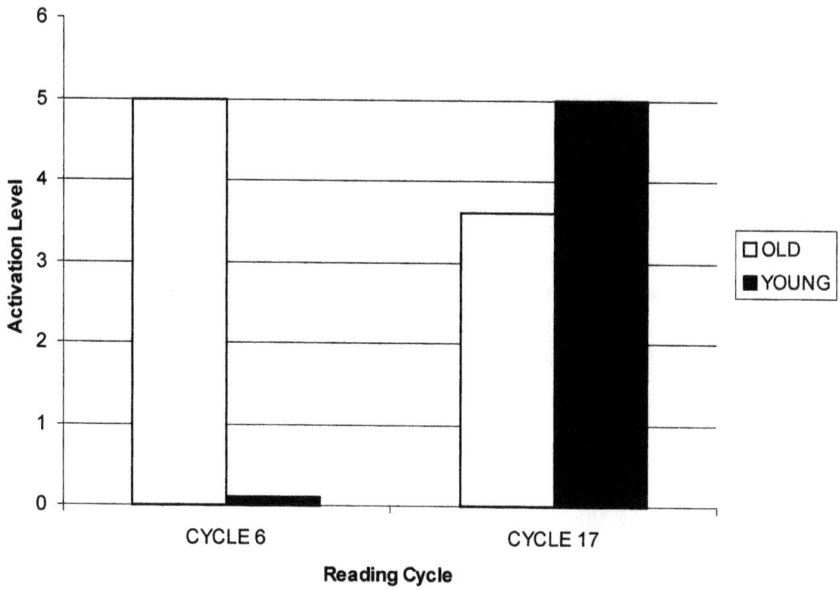

FIGURE 2 The Landscape model's simulated activation of "Old" and "Young" in the elaborated version of an inconsistent story at cycles 6 and 17.

Bill's physical condition (this reactivation is supported by the referential connection between 'he' and the earlier descriptions of the protagonist). The resulting activation patterns show that "young" and "old" are coactivated in cycle 17. The coactivation allows readers to detect the inconsistency between the two parts of the text.

The Landscape model simulation of how readers detect inconsistencies within a text matches behavioral data. Readers have longer reading times for target sentences when the information in the target sentence is inconsistent with the previous text (e.g., Albrecht & O'Brien, 1993; O'Brien, Rizzella, Albrecht, & Halleran, 1998). This effect occurred even when there was not a local coherence break in the text, indicating that readers are continually accessing their episodic memory representation of prior text even if the need for strategic reinstatement is low.

The conceptual framework of the Landscape model implies that an important factor influencing the likelihood that readers detect inconsistencies is how elaborately text information is encoded into the episodic memory representation. According to the Landscape model, the likelihood for the detection of an inconsistency depends on (a) the extent to which text information was activated and encoded in the earlier cycles, and how strongly it has become interconnected with other text concepts, and (b) the extent to which the later information overlaps, and is consistent, with the earlier memory trace.

To investigate these assumptions, a second simulation was run on a modification of the inconsistent text from Rizzella and O'Brien (1996). The modified and original versions of the inconsistent text differ in terms of how much is initially learned about the man, Bill. The elaborated version used in the first simulation contains several sentences of information pertaining to the age and physical condition of the man (see Appendix B) whereas the unelaborated version used in the second simulation contains only one such sentence. The second simulation was run on the unelaborated version of the inconsistent text to determine if inconsistency detection depends on how strongly Bill is encoded as a weak, old man in the reader's episodic memory representation.

The results of the simulation of the unelaborated version of the text are presented in Figure 3. As before, "old" is the label for the episodic memory representation and "young" represents information contained in the text at a later point. As shown in Figure 3, the reactivation of Bill as an old, weak man is much less than in the elaborated version of the text, reflecting the fact that this information is less strongly encoded in the episodic memory representation. As a result, the coactivation of 'old' and 'young' at cycle 17 is much less than it was in the simulation based on the elaborated version (see Figure 2), and likelihood of inconsistency detection is much less. Thus, according to the Landscape model, the strength of the memory trace and interconnectedness of the information about Bill being old and

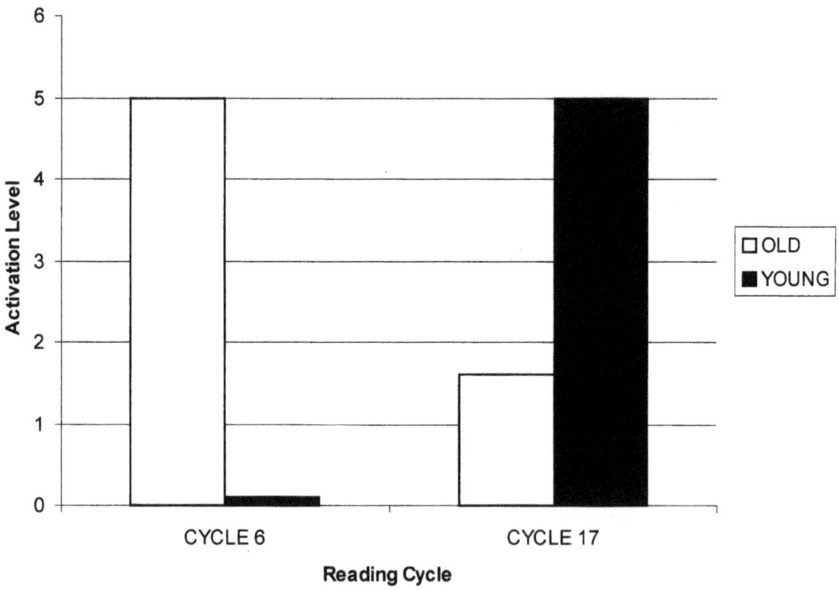

FIGURE 3 The Landscape model's simulated activation of "Old" and "Young" in the unelaborated version of an inconsistent story at cycles 6 and 17.

weak in the reader's episodic memory representation of the text affects the likelihood of inconsistency detection when the reader finds out later on that Bill is able to run quickly. The Landscape model's prediction that such early elaboration of information, and the resulting strengthening of its episodic memory representation, leads to increased likelihood of reactivation at later points in the text is consistent with findings of Rizzella and O'Brien (1996).

To summarize, cohort activation, and the interconnectedness of the reader's episodic memory representation, allows for the detection of an inconsistency and, hence, results in more processing time to resolve the inconsistency. Indeed, behavioral results, in terms of reading time data, exhibit this same pattern simulated by the Landscape model (Albrecht & O'Brien, 1993; O'Brien et al., 1998, Rizzella & O'Brien, 1996). Thus, central to the Landscape model simulation is the notion that readers' ability to detect an inconsistency in a text depends on the simultaneous activation of contradictory information in their developing episodic memory representation of the text.

CONCLUSION

The primary goal of this article was to describe a theoretical framework for investigating the availability of text elements during the process of reading. To achieve this goal, we have described and further validated a theoretical-computational model of reading, the Landscape model. Using two simulations of this model, we have shown that the Landscape model can accurately depict and explain the availability of text elements during two complex reading situations.

The architectural design of the Landscape model incorporates four main sources of activation: the text itself, carry-over from the preceding reading cycle, reactivation of prior text information, and information from the readers' background knowledge. The activation of concepts based on these sources can be either automatic or strategic. These sources result in fluctuations of activation as a reader proceeds through a text and interact dynamically with the reader's developing episodic memory representation of the text. The factors determining the activation values at each reading cycle depend on the cohort-activation parameter, a decay function, and an asymptotic learning rule. The model's power lies in its ability to combine theories and assumptions of the reading process, therefore allowing researchers to describe the potential availability of elements under specific reading conditions.

To demonstrate the utility of the Landscape model in tracking the availability of text elements, we described two simulations of different reading situations. The first simulation demonstrated that the Landscape model is able to track the availability of information when readers have different reading purposes and standards of coherence. In addition, this simulation shows that the model can accurately capture the reading of expository text. The second simulation demonstrated how the reader's developing episodic memory representation allows the detection of inconsistent text information. This simulation also shows how the role of various factors–such as elaboration and trace overlap–are depicted in the model and that have been found to influence that likelihood that readers detect inconsistencies. Thus, the Landscape model is shown to be an appropriate method for investigating the fluctuating activation of text ideas throughout the process of reading.

A unique property of the Landscape model is that its theoretical framework and architecture enable the simultaneous investigation of many different factors of reading. Prior studies often have investigated one text factor in isolation of other factors. The Landscape model provides a theoretical framework that integrates many factors of reading (e.g., different types of relations, standards of coherence, learning curves, etc.) in a single model. In addition, for practical reasons, most behavioral studies have only assessed the availability of concepts at a few points during reading. With the Landscape model, the activation of specific concepts can be tracked throughout the reading process rather than at only one or two points during reading. Thus, the Landscape model simulations incorporate multiple processes essential to reading throughout the entire reading of a text.

A second unique property of the Landscape model is that its computational implementation allows researchers to test their own hypotheses or alternative models. Although the Landscape model's architectural design is based on commonly executed processes and basic learning principles, the input parameters can be adjusted to test individual differences in readers (e.g., the size of working memory capacity, use of strategies, etc.) and to test alternative models. Thus, sources of activation, and their corresponding values, can be added or changed within the Landscape model based on a researcher's hypothesis about the processes that occur during text comprehension. For example, according to the Event–Indexing model readers maintain five standards of coherence when reading narrative discourse (Zwaan et al., 1995). The input parameters of the Landscape model can be modified to include each of these standards. Moreover, results of empirical studies suggest that some of these standards are more important to readers than others, so one might want to give each a different value. Likewise, other learning curves, cohort activation functions or parameters, etc., can be chosen. As a result, Landscape model simulations can be used to capture a whole family of reading models (the Construction–Integration model, Kintsch, 1998; the Event–Indexing Model, Zwaan et al., 1995; the 3CI model, Goldman & Varma, 1995, etc.) or theories about a particular reading phenomenon or both.

A third important contribution of the Landscape model is that it suggests mechanisms for phenomena that have been observed but not well-explained in behavioral studies. For example, according to the Landscape model different reading purposes result in different patterns of availability. Although prior behavioral studies have shown that different reading purposes produce different cognitive processes (e.g., Linderholm & van den Broek, 2002; van den Broek et al., 2001), there has been no explicit description of how these cognitive processes combine to affect the availability of concepts under different reading purposes. For example, some of the previous behavioral studies employed the verbal protocol method to determine what cognitive processes were executed by readers at each sentence. Yet, verbal protocol data were not able to show how the execution of particular cognitive processes at one sentence affects the availability of concepts at other sentences. The theoretical framework of the Landscape model provides potentially useful information about the availability of concepts as readers comprehend text beyond what researchers could thus far gather from behavioral studies.

Although we have shown that the Landscape model may be used to investigate the availability of text elements in two complex reading situations, the model would benefit from extensions. For example, one can think of reading as involving an external stimulus (i.e., the text) that directs attention and molds the reader's activations, in combination with the reader's own set of background knowledge and experiences. In this viewpoint of reading, the text is one of many sources of fluctuating activations (including real life, TV, conversations, etc.), which acts as a "set of directions for activations." Indeed, one can think of reading as a guided experience (Gerrig & McKoon, 1998). The Landscape model could be extended to simulate comprehension in other environments in addition to how comprehension occurs for written information.

Like other models of text comprehension, the Landscape model operates on text that has already been decoded and transformed into meaningful units. However, linguistic factors such as word decoding and, at a younger age, letter recognition (Gernsbacher, 1990; Perfetti, 1994) also influence the reading process. For example, compare the sentence, "The man threw the stone." with the sentence, "It was the man who threw the stone." Although the meaningful units are identical in both sentences, one could conceive that the "man" received more activation relative to other parts of the sentence in the second sentence than in the first sentence. Thus, the linguistic form in which a unit is presented can push the prominence of a particular concept within a sentence, influencing the distribution of activation within a reading cycle. The addition of linguistic aspects of the text presentation in the Landscape model, as well as in other computational models (e.g., the CI model), provides a promising future direction to study the availability of elements during text comprehension. Indeed, we expect such an incorporation of basic linguistic information into models of text comprehension an essential future development.

The Landscape model also has potential practical implications. One such implication is the identification of specific reading disabilities. Often it is difficult to pinpoint the exact source of a reader's disability. For example, the source of a reading disability may be a limited working memory capacity, the inability to easily access background knowledge, ineffective strategy use, and so on, or a combination of several factors. Limitations in any one of these factors would limit the availability, and eventual comprehension, of text information. By systematically altering the input parameters of the Landscape model (within the predetermined architecture), and comparing simulation results to actual behavioral output by readers with a disability, one may be able to identify a reader's specific difficulty and possibly tailor remediation to the needs of individual readers. Thus, the model may have important theoretical as well as practical implications.

ACKNOWLEDGMENTS

We thank David Rapp and Panayiota Kendeou for their comments on an earlier version of this article. This research was supported by the Golestan Foundation at the Netherlands Institute for the Advanced Study in the Humanities and Social Sciences, the Eva O. Miller fellowship, the Guy Bond Endowment for Reading and Literacy, the Center for Cognitive Sciences at the University of Minnesota through a grant from the National Institute of Child Health and Human Development (HD-07151), and the National Science Council, Taiwan, R. O. C. (NSC-90–2413-H-194-021).

REFERENCES

Albrecht, J., & O'Brien, E. (1993). Updating a mental model: Maintaining both local and global coherence. *Journal of Experimental Psychology: Learning, Memory, and Cognition, 19,* 1061–1070.

Bloom, C. P., Fletcher, C. R. van den Broek, P., Reitz, L., & Shapiro, B. P. (1990) An online assessment of causal reasoning during comprehension. *Memory & Cognition, 18,* 65–71.

Fletcher, C. R., & Bloom, C. P. (1988). Causal reasoning in the comprehension of simple narrative texts. *Journal of Memory and Language, 27,* 235–244.

Gernsbacher, M. A. (1989). Mechanisms that improve referential access. *Cognition, 32,* 99–156.

Gernsbacher, M. A. (1990). *Language comprehension as structure building.* Hillsdale, NJ: Lawrence Erlbaum Associates, Inc.

Gernsbacher, M. A. (1997). Attenuating interference during comprehension: The role of suppression. In D. L. Medin (Ed.), *The psychology of learning and motivation* (pp. 85–104). San Diego, CA: Academic.

Gerrig, R. J., & McKoon, G. (1998). The readiness is all: The functionality of memory-based text processing. *Discourse Processes, 26*(2–3), 67–86.

Goldman, S. R., & Saul, E. U. (1990). Flexibility in text processing: A strategy competition model. *Learning and Individual Differences, 2,* 181–219.

Goldman, S. R., & Varma, S. (1995). CAPping the construction-integration model of discourse comprehension. In C. A. Weaver, S. Mannes, & C. R. Fletcher (Eds.), *Discourse comprehension: Essays in honor of Walter Kintsch* (pp. 337–358). Mahwah, NJ: Lawrence Erlbaum Associates, Inc.

Graesser, A. C., Singer, M., & Trabasso, T. (1994). Constructing inferences during narrative text comprehension. *Psychological Review, 95,* 163–182.

Kintsch, W. (1988). The role of knowledge in discourse comprehension: A Construction-Integration Model. *Psychological Review, 95,* 163–182.

Kintsch, W. (1998). *Comprehension: A paradigm for cognition.* New York: Cambridge University Press.

Kintsch, W.A., & van Dijk, T.A. (1978). Toward a model of comprehension and production. *Psychological Review, 85*, 363–394.

Langston, M., & Trabasso, T. (1999). Modeling causal integration and availability of information during comprehension of narrative texts. In H. van Oostendorp & S. R. Goldman (Eds.), *The construction of mental representations during reading*, Mahwah, NJ: Lawrence Erlbaum Associates, Inc.

Linderholm, T., & van den Broek, P. (2002). The effects of reading purpose and working memory capacity limitations on the processing of expository texts. *Journal of Educational Psychology, 94*(4), 778–784.

Lorch, R. F., Jr., Lorch, E. P., & Klusewitz, M. A. (1993). College students' conditional knowledge about reading. *Journal of Educational Psychology, 85*, 239–252.

McKoon, G., & Ratcliff, R. (1992). Inferences during reading. *Psychological Review, 99*, 440–466.

Myers, J., & O'Brien, E. (1998). Accessing the discourse representation during reading. Discourse Processes, 26(2–3), 131–157.

Narvaez, D., van den Broek, P., & Ruiz, A. B. (1999). Reading purpose, type of text and their influence on think-alouds and comprehension measures. *Journal of Educational Psychology, 91*(3), 488–496.

O'Brien, E., Rizzella, M., Albrecht, J., & Halleran, J. (1998). Updating a situation model: A memory-based text processing view. *Journal of Experimental Psychology: Learning, Memory, & Cognition, 24*(5), 1200–1210.

Perfetti, C. (1994). Psycholinguistics and reading ability. In M. A. Gernsbacher (Ed.), *Handbook of psycholinguistics*. San Diego, CA: Academic.

Rizzella, M. L., & O'Brien, E. J. (1996). Accessing global causes during reading. *Journal of Experimental Psychology: Learning, Memory, and Cognition, 22*, 1208–1218.

Rizzella, M. L., & O'Brien, E. J. (2002). Retrieval of concepts in script-based texts and narratives: The influence of general world knowledge. *Journal of Experimental Psychology: Learning, Memory, and Cognition, 28*(4), 780–790.

Singer, M., & Ritchot, K. (1996). The role of working memory capacity and knowledge access in text inference processing. *Memory & Cognition, 24*, 733–743.

Trabasso, T., Secco, T. & van den Broek, P.W. (1984). Causal cohesion and story coherence. In H. Mandl, N.L. Stein, & T. Trabasso (Eds.), Learning and comprehension of text (pp 83–111). Mahwah, NJ: Lawrence Erlbaum Associates, Inc.

Trabasso, T., & Suh, S. (1993). Understanding text: achieving explanatory coherence through on-line inferences and mental operations in working memory. *Discourse Processes, 16*, 3–34.

van den Broek, P. (2002, July). *The landscape model.* Paper presented at the Twelfth Annual Meeting of the Society for Text and Discourse, Chicago.

van den Broek, P., Lorch, R. F., Linderholm, T., & Gustafson, G., (2001). The effect of readers' goals on the generation of inferences. *Memory & Cognition, 29*, 1081–1087.

van den Broek, P., Risden, K., Fletcher, C. R., & Thurlow, R. (1996). A "landscape" view of reading: Fluctuating patterns of activation and the construction of a stable memory representation. In B. K. Britton & A. C. Graesser (Eds.), *Models of understanding text* (pp. 165–187). Hillsdale, NJ: Lawrence Erlbaum Associates, Inc.

van den Broek, P., Risden, K., & Husebye-Hartmann, E. (1995). The role of readers' standards for coherence in the generation of inferences during reading. In R. F. Lorch, Jr., & E. J. O'Brien (Eds.), *Sources of coherence in text comprehension* (pp. 353–373). Hillsdale, NJ: Lawrence Erlbaum Associates, Inc.

van den Broek, P., Virtue, S., Everson, M., Tzeng, Y., & Sung, Y. (2002). Comprehension and memory of science texts: Inferential processes and the construction of a mental representation. In J. Otero, J. Leon, & A. C. Graesser (Eds.), *The psychology of science text comprehension* (pp. 131–154). Mahwah, NJ: Lawrence Erlbaum Associates, Inc.

van den Broek, P. W., Young, M., Tzeng, Y., & Linderholm, T. (1999). The landscape model of reading: Inferences and the on-line construction of a memory representation. In H. van Oostendorp & S. R. Goldman (Eds.), *The construction of mental representations during reading* (pp. 71–98). Mahwah, NJ: Lawrence Erlbaum Associates, Inc.

van Dijk, T., & Kintsch, W. (1983). *Strategies of Discourse Comprehension*. San Diego, CA: Academic.
Zwaan, R. A., Langston, M. C., & Graesser, A. C. (1995). The construction of situation models in narrative comprehension: An event-indexing model. *Psychological Science, 6*(5), 292–297.

APPENDIX A

Text used in the 'reading purpose' simulation: "Why American Songbirds are Vanishing" (from van den Broek et al., 2001)

1. The steep declines in waterfowl, shoreline birds, and grassland birds over the past several decades are generally well understood.

2. What is not as obvious is why forest-dwelling migratory songbirds are also vanishing; especially the so-called Neotropical migrants that breed in northern latitudes but migrate to winter homes in the tropics.

3. As reports of decreases in songbird populations accumulated, it was widely noted that the missing species could still be found in large continuous tracts of forests, but not in isolated tracts.

4. This observation was dubbed the "forest fragmentation effect."

5. What possible explanations might be given for the forest fragmentation effect?

6. One simple hypothesis to explain the forest fragmentation effect is that songbirds generally prefer larger forest plots as nesting sites and so avoid isolated plots because they tend to be small.

7. This hypothesis predicts that the density of songbirds' nests in a forest will increase as the size of the forest increases.

8. However, when researchers set about documenting the presence or absence of songbird species in forest fragments of different size, they obtained mixed and sometimes, contradictory results.

9. Another hypothesis is that many songbirds are averse to the edges of forests and reject small, isolated tracts because none of the habitat is far enough away from the edges.

10. There are good reasons why songbirds might want to nest away from the edge of a forest.

11. Forest margins are brighter, warmer, drier and windier than the interior and support more shrubs, vines and weeds.

12. This hypothesis was tested by observing the distribution of nesting territories in large forests that either surrounded a reservoir or had swaths cut to accommodate power-line rights-of-way.

13. The results of the test proved that the hypothesis was wrong.

14. A third hypothesis derives from the observation that the species whose numbers have declined most drastically are the long-distance, Neotropical migrants.

15. This hypothesis holds that tropical deforestation in South America (the winter home of the Neotropical migrants) is responsible for the declines, rather than fragmentation of the breeding habitat.

16. The hypothesis predicts that declines should be greatest for species that winter in regions undergoing rapid deforestation and least for species that winter in relatively unscathed parts of the tropics.

17. Comparisons of different species of Neotropical migrants do not support the hypothesis.

18. Two specific environmental changes have been identified that appear responsible for at least some of the decline in the songbird population.

19. First, the suburbs are havens for nest predators such as blue jays, raccoons and opossums, so the dwindling numbers of songbirds in isolated wood lots might be directly due to the activity of these animals.

20. To test this hypothesis, one scientist placed quail eggs in artificial nests and set them out in small, medium and large forests, and—for an undisturbed control site—in the Great Smoky Mountains National Park.

21. The results of the experiment confirmed the hypothesis.

22. The second factor responsible for the declining songbird population is an increase in nest parasites.

23. Parasitic birds lay their eggs in the nests of other species, who often raise the resulting offspring as their own.

24. Why would this reduce the number of songbirds?

25. A parasite's eggs typically hatch sooner than the eggs of its host, giving the hatchling parasite a head start over its nest mates.

26. By the time the host's eggs hatch, the parasite is so much bigger than the host's hatchlings that is obtains most of the food brought by the parents and the host's own offspring often starve.

27. A study in Wisconsin showed that 65% of the nests located near forest edges were parasitized by the cowbird.

28. The accessibility of isolated forest tracts to nest predators and parasites explains why the songbird populations are declining in these areas.

29. We must also account for the fact that the Neotropical migratory songbirds have declined so much more quickly than other songbirds.

30. In fact, it is not necessary to hypothesize a mechanism that selects the Neotropical birds out for special treatment because these migrants are naturally at a disadvantage in their breeding efforts.

31. The Neotropicals have a shorter breeding season and lay fewer eggs than other species.

32. Therefore, any environmental changes that reduce nesting success indiscriminately across all species would hit Neotropical migrants hardest because they have less margin for tolerance.

APPENDIX B

Elaborated text used in the 'inconsistent text' simulation (Rizzella & O'Brien, 1996)

1. Bill had always enjoyed walking in the early morning and this morning was no exception.
2. During his walks, he would stop to talk with some of his neighbors.
3. Bill had just celebrated his eighty-first birthday.
4. He didn't feel as strong as he was twenty years ago.
5. In fact, he began using a cane as he hobbled along on his morning walks.
6. He could not walk around the block without taking numerous breaks.
7. The neighborhood in which Bill lived was very small and friendly.
8. Everyone greeted him as he walked by each morning.
9. Bill especially liked to walk during the spring just when all of the flowers and trees were beginning to bloom.
10. He found it new and refreshing.
11. Today, Bill stopped to talk with Mrs. Jones.
12. They had been friends for quite sometime.
13. They were talking about how hot it had been.
14. For the past three months there had been record breaking high temperatures and no rain.
15. Soon there would be mandatory water rationing.
16. As Bill was talking to Mrs. Jones, he saw a young boy who was lying in the street hurt.
17. *He quickly ran and picked the boy up.*
18. *Bill carried the boy over to the curb.*
19. Although Bill helped the boy, Mrs. Jones ran into her house to call the boy's mother and an ambulance.
20. He kept the boy calm and still until help arrived.

For Product Safety Concerns and Information please contact our EU representative GPSR@taylorandfrancis.com
Taylor & Francis Verlag GmbH, Kaufingerstraße 24, 80331 München, Germany

www.ingramcontent.com/pod-product-compliance
Ingram Content Group UK Ltd.
Pitfield, Milton Keynes, MK11 3LW, UK
UKHW022121190926
475702UK00013B/1574
9780805895568